Unsafe Words

Q+ Public books are a limited series of curated volumes, inspired by the seminal journal *OUT/LOOK: National Lesbian and Gay Quarterly*. *OUT/LOOK* built a bridge between academic inquiry and the broader community. Q+ Public promises to revitalize a queer public sphere to bring together activists, intellectuals, and artists to explore questions that urgently concern all LGBTQ+ communities.

Series editors: E. G. Crichton, Jeffrey Escoffier (2018–2022)

Editorial Board

Unsafe Words

~

*Queering Consent in
the #MeToo Era*

EDITED BY
SHANTEL GABRIEAL BUGGS
AND TREVOR HOPPE

Rutgers University Press
New Brunswick, Camden, and Newark, New Jersey;
and London and Oxford, UK

Library of Congress Cataloging-in-Publication Data
Names: Buggs, Shantel Gabrieal, editor. | Hoppe, Trevor, 1983– editor.
Title: Unsafe words: queering consent in the #MeToo era /
edited by Shantel Gabrieal Buggs and Trevor Hoppe.
Description: New Brunswick, NJ: Rutgers University Press, [2023] |
Series: Q+ public | Includes bibliographical references and index.
Identifiers: LCCN 2022012277 | ISBN 9781978825406 (paperback) |
ISBN 9781978825413 (hardback) | ISBN 9781978825420 (epub) |
ISBN 9781978825444 (pdf)
Subjects: LCSH: Sex. | Sexual ethics | Sexual minorities. |
Sex crimes. | MeToo movement.
Classification: LCC HQ21 .U55 2023 | DDC 306.7—dc23/eng/20220401
LC record available at https://lccn.loc.gov/2022012277

A British Cataloging-in-Publication record for this book is available
from the British Library.

References to internet websites (URLs) were accurate at the time of writing.
Neither the author nor Rutgers University Press is responsible for URLs that
may have expired or changed since the manuscript was prepared.

∞ The paper used in this publication meets the requirements of the American
National Standard for Information Sciences—Permanence of Paper for
Printed Library Materials, ANSI Z39.48-1992.

www.rutgersuniversitypress.org

Manufactured in the United States of America

In Memory of
Mistress Velvet
And
Sexual Pioneers
Everywhere

Contents

Part 2: Responding to Sexual Harm

Series Foreword

Q+ Public is a series of small thematic books in which leading scholars, artists, community leaders and activists, independent writers and thinkers engage in critical reflection on contemporary LGBTQ political, social and cultural issues.

Why Q+ Public? It invites all of the L, the G, the B, the T, the Q, and any other sexual and gender minorities. It asserts the need and existence of a Queer public space. It is also a riff on "John Q. Public" stripped of his gender, and even on Star Trek's Q Continuum! Q+ Public is about elevating the challenges of thinking about gender, sex, and sexuality in contemporary life.

Q+ Public is an outgrowth, after a long hibernation, of *OUT/LOOK Lesbian and Gay Quarterly*, a pioneering political and cultural journal that sparked intense national debate during the time it was published in San Francisco, 1988 to 1992. *OUT/LOOK*, in turn, spawned the *OutWrite* conferences that started in San Francisco in 1990 and 1991, then moved to Boston for a number of years.

We plan to revive *OUT/LOOK*'s political and cultural agenda in a new format. We aim to revitalize a queer public sphere in which to explore questions that urgently concern all LGBTQ communities. The movement that started with Stonewall was built on the struggles for political and civil rights of people of color, women, labor unions, and the disabled. These struggles led, unwittingly, to a major reconfiguration of the sex/gender system. The world of Stonewall was fading, and the new queer world was being born.

Our first books in this series address themes of queering consent, queer archive interventions, and whether PrEP is a pill for promiscuity. Each book finds a way to dive into the deep nuances and discomforts of each topic. Other books on the struggle for LGBTQ K–12 curriculum, the intersection of race and gender, transgenerational performance, and the incarceration of people with AIDS are in preparation.

We anticipate future volumes on shifting lesbian, queer and trans identities; immigration, race, and homophobia; queer aging and the future of queer communities; new forms of community-based queer history; and LGBTQ politics after marriage, to name a few. Each book features multiple points of view, strong art, and a strong editorial concept.

In this era of new political dangers, Q+ Public takes on the challenges we face and offers a forum for public dialogue.

Unsafe Words ventures into territory that very few academic books dare tread. In a world where the discourses on sexuality are carefully tailored to reinforce morality, this collection of essays assembles reflections that go beyond the reductive idea of "consent" as "yes saying" that has become the dominant mode of regulating sexual life in the wake of #MeToo. Taking its guidance from queer social life and practices in kink communities, the book maps how ethical sex can both address the racial, sexual, and gendered contexts of sex and the realities of desire and pleasure.

E. G. Crichton
Jeffrey Escoffier

Unsafe Words

Introduction

SHANTEL GABRIEAL BUGGS AND TREVOR HOPPE

In April 1982, some forty years before the publication of this collection, a group of feminist scholars and activists met at Barnard College for a controversial gathering. The conference, titled "Towards a Politics of Sexuality," aimed to inject pleasure back into feminist discourses on sexuality for women. Women against Pornography picketed the event, angered by the perceived tolerance of pornography and sado-masochism (SM) of the conveners. Many of the essays in the volume that resulted from the event—1992's *Pleasure and Danger*, edited by Carole S. Vance—remain relevant today.[1] As Vance states in its introduction, "To only focus on pleasure and gratification ignores the patriarchal structure in which women act, yet to speak only of sexual violence and oppression ignores women's experience with sexual agency and choice and unwittingly increases the sexual terror and despair in which women live."[2]

Vance's edited volume remains a powerful exploration of the fraught tensions between pleasure and danger. It frames sexual harm through the lens of patriarchy and the gender binary. Women—from the married heterosexual to the radical lesbian and the so-called promiscuous—are deservedly front and center as the book tackles how male violence does harm to many groups. Similar critiques of consent and men's sexual entitlement appear in Joseph Fischel's *Screw Consent*, where he concludes that powerful men's successful efforts to constrain women's legal autonomy and access is more pressing an issue than whether the sex is necessarily consensual.[3] Amia Srinivasan's *The Right to Sex* similarly argues that, under patriarchy, simplistic notions of consent as a clear matter of yes or no and calls to "Believe women" are blunt tools that fail to fully grasp the politics of sex.[4]

We write this introduction thirty years after *Pleasure and Danger* and cannot help but note how much remains the same, despite worthy interventions from scholars and mainstream writers alike. The battles over pleasure and danger remain fierce. Just turn on the nightly news to witness the impact #MeToo activists have had in ushering in an era of reckoning and accountability for one powerful man after another. Or glance at the latest viral story on social media, where fictional short stories no longer seem like fiction when exploring the discomfort of navigating sex.[5] Other, more troubling aspects of these developments also feel familiar. The women who have become the face of this contemporary movement—a movement founded by a Black woman, Tarana Burke—are overwhelmingly white and assumed to be exclusively heterosexual. The Western focus of #MeToo (and perhaps even much of this volume) silences the work of feminists in and from the Global South.[6] When we note how much has remained the same we must also contend with how the long arms of structural racism, anti-Blackness, and empire have facilitated such a circumstance.

The radical (yet unrealized) potential of this moment leaves us wondering: What does #MeToo mean for queer communities? Vance argued that the pleasure/danger dichotomy was too simplistic to fully theorize women's sexual experiences, which in her words were "more complicated, more difficult to grasp, more unsettling."[7] As the chapters in this book reveal, the sexual lives of queer people, too, are more complicated than a straightforward binary of either pleasurable or dangerous activity. Some queers seek safety in sex while others do not; for some, sex can be a means to explore various ways of being outside of a heteronormative *and* homonormative world. So, when we ask what the #MeToo moment means for queer folks, what we are really asking is both what can the #MeToo moment teach queer people about consent and what can queers contribute to this ongoing conversation in a way that does not erase their queerness. If queer relationships are necessarily marked by differently gendered power dynamics (as well as racialized and classed dynamics), how is all this power negotiated?

It is important to say at the outset that when we use the word "queer" in this collection, we do not use it as a synonym for same-gender or same-sex relationships. Rather, this collection considers a broader array of non-heteronormative sexual relations. This includes not just gay men, lesbians, bisexuals, and trans people but also those who practice kink and BDSM (shorthand for bondage, domination, submission, and masochism), engage in public sex, or participate in sex work. We are interested in "queering" consent by working through how people can, and do, disentangle consent from heteronormative logics. Within these outsider sexual cultures, even sex between cisgender men and women partners has the potential to disrupt fundamental heteronormative assumptions about sex: that sex should be had in private, that it should not be traded for money, and that sex should be egalitarian and pursued for reproduction—or, perhaps, pleasure—but certainly not pain.

This collection tackles these issues in two sections, revealing who #MeToo can *and should* include while also issuing calls not simply to end sexual violence but also to set people and their communities on a path toward healing.

The first section titled "Queering Consent" considers the nature of consent and power. What does it mean to consent to sex? How does consent look different in queer sex spaces? What tools might help us practice sex more ethically? And how does power shape sexual consent in queer and trans contexts that go beyond a (perhaps oversimplified) feminist lens of patriarchal oppression and submission? How do you negotiate and practice consent when one partner is more dominant or in a socially more powerful position? Can queer sex be consensual when that power imbalance is extreme?

The second section, titled "Responding to Sexual Harm," debates how queer communities ought to evaluate and eventually redress sexual harm. What does it mean to hold each other accountable? How do we do that when the seemingly obvious system of recourse—the U.S. criminal justice system—is a site of racial, gender-based, and sexual violence? How do we even recognize when we have been harmed or when we have harmed others? What do we potentially risk in terms of our understandings of safety when we prioritize an abolitionist and transformative justice approach?

Though not exhaustive, we hope these two sections guide engagement. But we also recognize that this structure—power and consent versus sexual harm—imposes artificial boundaries and limitations that the contributors of this volume are all working to resist either through content, theorizing, methodology, or form. Truly, any of the pieces in the volume can speak to concerns addressed in either section. Therefore, our efforts to structure the unstructured is less to force the voices of our contributors into an acceptable form and more to provide a roadmap for how to navigate this text, much in the same way that contributors to this volume are sharing insights on how to navigate the unwieldy dynamics of the pleasures and dangers of sex, sensuality, and queer space.

The perspectives included in this volume are not only shaped by our imposed structuring; these essays are also shaped by varied social positioning. The experiences of white cisgender gay men and lesbians do not neatly map onto the experiences of Black trans femmes, and this volume has no expectations that these essays and experiences should be considered interchangeable or as speaking for all LGBTQIA+ people. What we offer in this volume is a variety of perspectives to open the door for further debate, for critical engagement with the ways that the consent–nonconsent binary can and often does fail.

Queering Consent

#MeToo has reignited debates about sexual ethics, primarily this burning question: What does it mean to consent? Queer social theorist Judith Butler has argued that answering this question is more complicated that it seems. Consent is not a binding contract. Agreeing to have sex does not entitle your partner to do whatever they want. Partners are constantly renegotiating what they each want, live, in the moment. "Indeed," Butler writes, "it may be that one thing adults do when we consent to a sexual encounter or relation is to try and understand what it means to consent or, rather, to explore some regions of 'yes saying'—agreeing, affirming, willingness to try, the fear of trying, probing, wishing, and dreaming."[8]

Communication is only part of the equation. To Angela Jones (she/they),[9] nobody knows this better than sex workers. In chapter 1, Jones reflects both on her own experiences as a stripper and on research interviews she conducted with sex workers to understand how professionals do consent.

Although clear communication is a good first step, it is not a panacea. Power dynamics can complicate sexual agreements, especially for sex workers with marginalized identities. Jones writes, "Discussing one's needs is vital, but sexual scripts, cultural mores, stereotypes, and power relations shape the articulation of sexual needs and boundaries. Especially for those who are economically vulnerable, [sex workers] may make choices that can put them at risk, but such coping strategies help them navigate imbalanced power relationships."

Jones concludes her chapter by critically reflecting on recent attempts to promote consent as "sexy." But although these efforts may be well intentioned, she argues that they are misguided: "Conversations regarding consent do not always feel sexy at all. They can feel awkward, weird, uncomfortable, and yes, downright mood-killing, especially when they occur during sex." The only way to truly end sexual violence would be to dismantle the structural systems—the patriarchy, transmisogyny, and white supremacy—that enable it.

Jones joins several authors in this volume in criticizing recent efforts to reimagine consent in the wake of #MeToo. In both their chapters, Alex Cheves (he/him) and Trevor Hoppe (he/him) take issue with "enthusiastic consent." Although definitions vary, some argue that consent requires both parties to verbally ask and agree to each sexual act. In some queer sex spaces, however, verbal communication is nearly taboo. To this point, one of the editors of this volume recently received an email from a friend that was an invitation to an orgy in Chicago, with these words: "Finish off the weekend—and yourself—at this support group with lots of sharing but very little speaking."[10] This invite reflects the social norms of gay orgies or bathhouses, where there is often a tacit agreement that conversation ought to be kept to a minimum. No one wants to kill the vibe.

In chapter 2, Alexander Cheves reflects on having sex in a similar context: a nearly pitch-black backroom with music so loud that conversation is impossible and, in practice, frowned on. In that context, consent certainly doesn't look like a polite exchange in which Botticelli-esque lovers quietly ask, "Do you like it when I stroke your nipples like this?" The language of consent in the bathhouse is often not spoken but instead is performed through a ritual of eye contact and nods, monosyllabic mouth-noises (e.g., "Mmm . . ." "nice," "sup"), and nudges.

"Yes saying" is especially complicated in bathhouses and other queer sex spaces in which pushing a partner's boundaries is a desired feature of erotic exchange. Cheves reflects on a partner who pushed him to do something he was not sure he was ready for just yet. Trevor Hoppe reflects on a partner who was much more aggressive and dominant in bed than had been arranged. Both authors enjoyed the experiences immensely, yet were left reflecting on the need for unique tools for negotiating consent in such boundary-pushing contexts.

Hoppe points out that "enthusiastic consent" can be useful in an education environment, like how we teach young people to follow the speed limit in driver's ed. "We teach teenagers in driver's ed to follow the speed limit and to always keep their hands at 9 and 3. But let's face it: every driver's ed teacher knows that most (if not all) of their students will wind up speeding and occasionally driving with their knees." Some advocates, however, go further to insist that any sex that diverges from the enthusiastic model is necessarily assault, effectively "labeling nearly all the sex ever had in the world as assault. And if everything is assault, then nothing is."

Enthusiastic consent may be a useful education tool, but it is not a yardstick for assessing harm. Hoppe's reflections on his sexual experiences as a white cisgender gay man inform his discussion of the tools he needed for practicing ethical sex.

Jane Ward (she/her) continues in this vein in chapter 4 by revealing the heteronormative underpinnings of the enthusiastic consent model. Ward points out that enthusiastic consent is a corrective against men's selfishness and the dearth of pleasure women experience in heterosexual sex. In short, enthusiastic consent is "understandably anchored in straight women's experiences of heteropatriarchal sex." Should a concept built on the back of heteronormativity be copied and pasted into lesbian and other queer sexual cultures?

Ward argues that "lesbians and other queers . . . have long asserted our right to re-code and re-gender nonreciprocal sex." She points to the lesbian figure of the "pillow princess," or a femme whose sexual role is to receive pleasure but to never give it. Her counterpart, the "stone butch," is tasked with pleasuring their femme partner but never receiving it themselves. Far from just parroting heterosexual sex roles, this butch/femme model turns the masculine partner into the pleasure giver and the feminine one as the pleasure receiver. In this context, Ward argues that heteronormative models of enthusiastic consent are "less of a guiding star for queer women."

In chapter 5, Gloria González-López (she/her) and Anahi Russo Garrido (she/they) consider how consent operates in lesbian relationships in Mexico City. Reflecting on Garrido's findings from fieldwork in the city, they discuss how lesbian couples negotiate what's allowed or permissible with women outside the relationship. These "*pequeños permisos*" (little permissions) allow couples to maintain boundaries within the relationship while also offering a certain degree of freedom—such as making out with other women at the bar. Their dialogue helps reveal how these debates and discussions about power, sexual freedom, and autonomy can play out differently depending on religion, situational consent, and the presence of abuse. In particular, González-López and Russo Garrido thoughtfully illustrate the failings of Western lenses when trying to grasp the notion of consent.

The late, iconic Mistress Velvet (she/they) contributed an essay to this collection (chapter 6) before they died that speaks to the special complexities for Black femme dominatrices working with mostly high-powered, cisgender white male clients. Velvet became internationally famous in 2018 when mainstream media interviews highlighted their practice of requiring white male clientele to pay reparations and read Black feminist theory before being dominated by them.[11] They write:

> My domination may take many forms, but its foundations lie in a race play that focuses on the ownership and enslavement of white men. This literal playing with and disruption of standard racial comforts and scripts work in conjunction with my femdom to upset systems of straight, cisgender, white male hegemony; it lurks on the fringes of erotic performativity—a perversion rife with history and trauma.

Mistress Velvet's essay speaks powerfully to how racial trauma and histories of violence show up in our erotic lives in unexpected and sometimes challenging ways. As they noted in a 2020 interview in *The Black Scholar*, "We [Black Dommes] are literally perverting specific racial and gendered dynamics. Black women are oppressed. We don't have global power. But we are inverting this within BDSM. We are prototypes."[12]

We remain devastated that Mistress Velvet is no longer with us. When they agreed to write for this collection early on in our process, both of us literally exclaimed for joy. We so admired their tenacious willingness to *literally* fuck the cishet, white patriarchy and their deep commitment to activism around reproductive justice, gender violence, housing inequality, and LGBTQ+ inclusive sexual health and relationship education. We hope that their legacy and spirit live on in some small way through this collection. We dedicate it to their memory.

Before they passed, we were truly lucky to be able to arrange a photoshoot of Mistress Velvet to include in Don (D. S.) Trumbull's (he/him) photo essay, which concludes part I. His photo essay beautifully visualizes themes that run throughout this book and especially this first part: power, seduction, community, and intimacy. We include these stunning photos to offer readers a visual moment of reflection.

As the chapters in this section demonstrate, crafting a universal theory of consent is a fraught project. Yet, despite our different perspectives, every contributor to this volume shares a commitment to promoting consent. We recognize that different people and communities will need different tools to practice sex safely and ethically. Safe words are not for everyone; nor will the recently popularized model of "enthusiastic consent" work for everyone. But we all agree that when consent breaks down, sex can become violent, and the results—long-lasting emotional, psychological, and potentially physical damage—can be devastating.

Authors in this book poke and prod in search of more capacious, queer, and kink-friendly notions of consent. We do this in the spirit of finding more tools and more language to promote better, more ethical, and more pleasurable sex.

Responding to Sexual Harm

When consent breaks down or is otherwise violated, how can queer communities imagine different responses to sexual harm? In the book's second section, authors consider the unique challenges faced by queer spaces and communities in responding to harm. The first four chapters look inward to our own communities and point to the failures of queer spaces to protect our own from sexual violence. The final two chapters look outside our communities to U.S. law enforcement, a fundamentally flawed system that the authors argue is a pillar of American structural racism, transmisogyny, and heteronormativity. These six chapters ask and answer questions at the heart of this volume: How can our communities imagine different responses to sexual violence that do not depend on the law to serve justice?

Chapters in part I reveal how different queer sexual cultures and spaces operate with different rules of engagement. What is considered normative in one space is violative in another, and vice versa. But as Blu Buchanan (they/them) notes in chapter 8, not all participants who go into queer sexual spaces are aware of these unspoken and unwritten rules. Drawing on the work of Samuel Delany, as well as their own experiences in bathhouses as a light-skinned Black nonbinary femme, they reflect on moments when consent breaks down. They search for a way to conceptualize consent in these spaces not as an individual responsibility but instead as a community-level good: "Resisting neoliberal deployments of consent, community consent identifies nonconsensual encounters between actors as a breakdown and harm to the community as a whole." They argue for doing the transformative justice work needed to promote community consent within public sex spaces.

Many LGBTQ communities struggle with how to respond to sexual violence. We too often ignore the problem or engage in victim-blaming behavior that inflicts even more harm and certainly does little to help us collectively. Many times, queer nightclub spaces facilitate violations of bodily autonomy that blur lines between wanted and unwanted attention. In chapter 9, Shantel Gabrieal Buggs (she/her) notes the double bind of being a queer woman of color whose fat, racialized, and sexualized body seemingly "invites" being touched. She struggles to balance desires to reject that invasion and to protect her fellow queers from carceral responses. This blurriness makes queer nightclub spaces confusing and potentially unsafe. She asks that we contend with the ways that we socialize certain people to believe they must allow their bodies to be accessible lest they be labeled "bad queers." We must do better precisely because so many of us need our LGBTQ communities so urgently.

In chapter 10, James McMaster (he/him) continues this line of inquiry by reflecting on his experiences as a gay Asian man navigating consent in gay bars. What is the line between harmless fun and assaultive behavior? How does race play a role in structuring his interactions with others? He thinks back to recent experiences at such a bar:

> Consider this: I'm at Elixir and another gaysian wraps his arms around me. I don't consent to this, but they seem tipsy, friendly, and harmless enough so I giggle and wiggle away. That same night, someone—I don't see who—grabs my ass. This act in a straight bar might cross a line, but does it here? Does the race of the grabber matter? Does the fact that I was more flattered than offended make it okay?

He asks these questions, he says, "earnestly, not rhetorically," striving to imagine a "gaysian sexual ethics."

Many authors in this collection struggle with whether and how to define experiences in their own lives as harmful. Mark King (he/him) writes in chapter 11 about such an experience from a unique angle: as a potential perpetrator. As a white gay man who came of age in the 1970s, he began hooking up with older men while in his early teens. Without giving too much away, he reflects on one encounter in which he pressured a much older man into having sex with him. He looks back on this encounter, which left his partner in tears, and asks, "Was I a teenage sexual predator?" His essay flips conventional perspectives on the power imbalance of intergenerational sex as it reflects on an experience in which King felt like he was not a victim but an instigator—even, perhaps, a culpable manipulator. Although this book does not and cannot begin to resolve the complexities raised by young people having sex, King's chapter points readers to ethical quandaries raised by framing sexual consent through age categories.

When we experience sexual violence, what can be done to seek justice? The final two essays consider the serious problems with the U.S. criminal justice system. V. Jo Hsu (they/them) argues in chapter 12 that the law itself is a sexist, racist, homophobic, and transphobic system that inflicts its own violence on us. They remind us that "policing and prisons were designed to elicit obedience under white heteropatriarchal governance, and they continue to target people of color, disabled people, transgender and queer folks, particularly those who live at the intersections of those identities." Hsu argues that we must find alternative pathways to healing that do not primarily rely on the criminal justice system.

In a concluding interview that Trevor conducted, Dominique Morgan (she/her) echoes many of Hsu's concerns. What is justice? How do we as queer and trans people hope to achieve it? Morgan argues that U.S. law does not and cannot offer us justice. As a Black trans woman, as an executive director of a national queer abolitionist organization (Black and Pink), and as a victim of sexual violence herself, Morgan reflects on the failures of our legal institutions. The law never protected her. Quite the opposite: while serving time in prison, she experienced sexual assault at the hands of a correctional officer. She notes, "The most protected I have ever felt was as an abolitionist who leaned on community and not systems. I'm going to keep on leaning on community."

Toward a Queer Politics of Consent

Taken together, the essays in this collection highlight many issues facing queer, trans, and nonbinary people as we work to build ethical, sex-positive communities. Queer folks have long been leaders in radically rethinking the possibilities of sexual intimacy. In many ways, we are pioneers in pleasure, turning one antiquated and heteronormative idea about sex after another on its head.

The title of this collection—*Unsafe Words*—speaks to a specific innovation pioneered by queer people and kink practitioners that is custom built for non-normative sex. Safe words are usually prearranged and unlikely to ever come up in a particular scene (a flower-loving friend of one of the editor's uses "bougainvillea," for instance). Safe words are unique because they allow a partner (usually but not always the submissive partner) to set boundaries. They are empowered to decide when a scene gets too heavy or they want to stop. But safe words also are unique in that they allow space to play. You may begin an experience thinking you are not willing or interested in a particular practice, but with the right partner, in the right moment, you may find yourself open to it. Having a safe word can allow you to let your partner(s) push you to new sexual frontiers while always having an exit button at hand.

Through such innovation and creative sexual play, queer sexual cultures have greatly expanded what is sexually possible and, to an extent, permissible. And yet we are still living, loving, and fucking within the same world as our (mostly) heterosexual counterparts. We still must exist in a society that does not flinch at showing mass carnage, rape, and murder on television but loses their collective mind when Janet Jackson reveals the outline of her breast at the Super Bowl halftime show. TV series and movies feature a highly sanitized version of sex that is only experienced by the young and extremely beautiful. Although butts and breasts are a dime a dozen these days on screen, we cannot remember *ever* seeing a clitoris on cable television or in a non-R-rated film—and rarely do we catch even a glimpse of a flaccid penis (unless it is an episode of *Euphoria*). Finding porn that does not center male, white, physically fit, and young bodies can be challenging; friends of one of the editors often lament the ubiquitous pink nipples to be found in lesbian pornography—with Black people siloed in "ebony" porn.

Sex is seemingly *everywhere*. Yet most of us lack the vocabulary to have a serious conversation about what turns us on (or what turns us off). For queer people, the problem is made worse because we do not see ourselves reflected in the highly sexualized media that do exist.

Sex education for most Americans consists of a stern lecture about abstinence, pregnancy prevention, and scared-straight–style sexually transmitted infection programming. In such a curriculum, pleasure does not exist, especially for queers. This sexual "education" focuses primarily on penetrative, penis-in-vagina sex and certainly does not entertain the fact that not all people with penises are men and not all people with vaginas are women. Beyond ignoring a diversity of anatomy, we are also not given much to consider in terms of attraction or practice: try asking a high school teacher how to know if you are more of a top or a bottom; if you are bisexual, pansexual, or asexual; or if you are a dom(me) or a sub.

We are not taught how to fuck.
We are not taught how to have the best sex of our lives.
We are not taught how to explore the difference between
     uncomfortable and harmful sex.
We are not taught how to demand the sex we want—the sex
     we *deserve*.
We are not taught the many ways to say yes.
And, perhaps most devastatingly, we are not taught how to
     say *no*.
Shame and silence promote violence—*not consent.*

Although the title of the book is an homage to safe words, it is also a reference to the fact that the kind of explicit sexual talk inside these pages remains deeply taboo. We believe that queer communities ought to be leading examples in promoting and practicing nuanced, fluid, and *consensual* sex. We believe the essays in this book are a step in that direction. We hope you will join us in envisioning and enacting a transformed consent expansive enough to encompass all the pleasures that queerness invites. As Srinivasan so clearly articulates, we do not *know* the future of sex, but we can imagine and hope for a world that is different.

Notes

1. For a contextual review of that collection, see Arlene Stein and Andrea Press, "Reviewed Work: *Pleasure & Danger: Exploring Female Sexuality* by Carole S. Vance," *Berkeley Journal of Sociology* 30 (1985): 205–212.

2. Carole Vance, "Pleasure and Danger: Towards a Politics of Sexuality," in *Pleasure and Danger: Exploring Female Sexuality* (Boston: Routledge, 1984), 1.

3. Joseph Fischel, *Screw Consent: A Better Politics of Sexual Justice* (Oakland: University of California Press, 2019).

4. Amia Srinivasan, *The Right to Sex: Feminism in the Twenty-First Century* (New York: Farrar, Straus and Giroux, 2021).

5. Kristen Roupenian's *New Yorker* short story, "Cat Person," caused an internet firestorm in 2017 for its depiction of uncomfortable and unsatisfying sex and harassment tied up with a potentially manipulative age gap; it caused more controversy in 2021 when it was found that Roupenian seemed to have lifted aspects of someone's real life without their consent: Roupenian, "Cat Person," *The New Yorker*, December 4, 2017, https://www.newyorker.com/magazine/2017/12/11/cat-person; Alexis Nowicki, "'Cat Person' and Me," *Slate*, July 8, 2021, https://slate.com/human-interest/2021/07/cat-person-kristen-roupenian-viral-story-about-me.html.

6. Vrushali Patil and Jyoti Puri, "Colorblind Feminisms: Ansari-Grace and the Limits of #MeToo Counterpublics," *Signs: Journal of Women and Culture in Society* 46, no. 3 (2021): 689–713; Lila Abu-Lughod, "Do Muslim Women Really Need Saving? Anthropological Reflections on Cultural Relativism and Its Others," *American Anthropologist* 104, no. 3 (2002): 783–790.

7. Carole Vance, "Pleasure and Danger: Towards a Politics of Sexuality," in *Pleasure and Danger: Exploring Female Sexuality* (Boston: Routledge, 1984), 5.

8. Judith Butler, "Consent: Some Thoughts on Psychoanalysis and Law," *Columbia Journal of Gender and the Law* 21, no. 2 (2012): 3–27, 20.

9. We note the preferred pronouns of all contributors in the introduction after the first mention of their name.

10. Email invitation forwarded to the author for a Chicago sex party, "Athletic Support Group," on May 23, 2021.

11. See, for example, Amanda Duberman, "Meet the Dominatrix Who Requires the Men Who Hire Her to Read Black Feminist Theory," *Huffington Post*, February 13, 2018. https://www.huffpost.com/entry/mistress-velvet_n_5a822b50e4b00ecc923d4eba.

12. Kirin Wachter-Grene, "Caretaking in So Many Ways: A Conversation with Mistress Velvet," *Black Scholar: Journal of Black Studies and Research* 50, no. 2 (2020): 43–47.

PART 1

Queering Consent

1

Sex Workers Are Experts on Sexual Consent

ANGELA JONES

People seeking conceptual or ethical guidance on consent should be talking to sex workers: they are the leading experts on negotiating consent in sexual encounters.[1] Yet, they are too often left out of liberal feminist discussions of sex and consent, which tend to center the stories and narratives of straight, cisgender white women facing patriarchal sexual violence in their interactions with straight cis men.[2] Like Tarana Burke, the Black woman who founded #MeToo in 2006, and other Black survivors, sex workers were left out of the debates surrounding #MeToo and consent that barreled onto the scene in 2018.[3]

In this chapter, I use insights from sex work to explore the nuances of consent. Yes, consent is an agreement to engage in sex. However, consent is also about communication. In discussions of consent and warding off lousy sex and preventing sexual assault, consent is often framed around questions such as these: Did they say yes? Was it affirmative or enthusiastic? Did the person withdraw their consent at any time? And so on. Of course, these are vital questions. However, in addition to affirming that one wants to have sex, discussing what one consents to is just as necessary.

As a researcher, when I interview people I give them detailed information about the study's goals, what role they will play, the benefits and risks to them of participation, and what they can expect from me. In other words, I acquire informed consent. The same should be true of sexual encounters. People need to know to what they are consenting. Sex workers negotiate consent for a living. Although engaging in serious negotiations in noncommercial sexual encounters can feel transactional, sex workers show us how and why such discussions are critical. Moreover, they show us that reducing the incidence of terrible sex and sexual assault requires more than merely better communication: existing power relationships and systems of inequality shape interpersonal exchanges in ways that complicate agreements for sex.

Throughout my research on sex work, I've had the opportunity to survey and interview a wide range of sex workers laboring in the camming industry, traditional pornography, pro-domme work, and full-service escorting. I also have a background in sex work. The negotiation of boundaries with clients is a fundamental part of a sex worker's labor. These discussions help keep them safe and promote more pleasurable work experiences. Through the lens of sex work, I discuss four themes regarding consent that can be extrapolated to noncommercial sexual encounters: (1) consent is not one size fits all, (2) existing power arrangements matter, (3) technology is your friend, and (4) consent is not incredibly sexy.

Consent Is Not One Size Fits All

After the flood of sexual assault and #MeToo stories that dominated mainstream media in late 2017 and 2018,[4] articles on dating and consent soon inundated the press.[5] Mainstream articles provided readers with advice for negotiating consent[6] and even presented lists of thirty-five ways to ask for consent.[7] However, consent is not one size fits all.[8] In what follows, I explore how both client/partner subjectivity and worker/self shape the communication and articulation of boundaries and desires in discussions of consent.

CLIENTS: WHO YOU ARE FUCKING MATTERS

Sexual consent is complicated, and context shapes the ways we negotiate. In the late 1990s, I worked as a stripper and also saw a few regulars outside the club. As an exotic dancer, the ways I'd discuss the terms of a lap dance or a trip to the champagne room were different based on the customer.[9] Generally, with older white men, whom I mistrusted more than others, my terms were more stringent. My script for them might be, "I'm gonna tease you so good, you'll never wanna leave—but, remember, no touching baby." If I found a customer attractive or knew they were a whale (a big spender), the terms might change. In the context of the lap-dance room, I might say, "Ya know, the more I dance, the more I get into it, and the more excited I get. If you let me dance for you for four songs, I'll let you use your hands and show you where you can touch me." In the notoriously scandalous champagne room, visits required even more direct negotiations (see endnote 9 for an example). Although, in the 1990s, there were much fewer women customers than today, my negotiations about consensual touching and even kissing were far less rigid with them. Honestly, I often failed to articulate the boundaries with women customers.

For the clients I saw outside the club, I also negotiated the terms of our ongoing relationships differently based on the individual. For example, in the club, Roger had to pay me $1,200 plus money showers[10] on stage and pay for my drinks, of course, just to sit with him on a Saturday night. We had clearly defined and communicated rules that structured our relationship in the club. Outside the club our relationship was different and required different terms.

I was not at all attracted to Roger. He was a much older, white cis man. In fact, I remember feeling repulsed when he kissed me or touched my breasts. Thus, with him, I made clear that my "girlfriend experience"[11] included dinner dates, but that when he dropped me home, he could not come upstairs to my apartment, and I would only make out with him in the car. He eventually tired of this and moved on to another dancer. I, too, moved on to a different relationship with a client named Luis.

With Luis, it was different. He was a person of color, and he was kind. Oh, and he really liked me. In hindsight, there was definitely some "captain save a hoe"[12] psychology at play, but I didn't feel objectified by him. Thus, I was open to full-service dates with him and to hosting at my home. We discussed that I would be his girlfriend for hire in exchange for expensive dinners, apartment rental payments, cash, and gifts. I have this fond memory of one night we spent at City Island in the Bronx, eating and dancing and genuinely having a fantastic time. The payoff for my sex work was not only monetary. Given that I had negotiated terms that made me feel comfortable, valued, respected, and in control, I was able to enjoy the time I spent with Luis—even though it *was* work.

In my research, I explored with full-service providers how different contexts and types of clients shaped their consent negotiations. Devon, a 20-year-old Black agender escort, highlighted these points:

> I require that people wear condoms. Just because I am not on birth control. So, I am just on testosterone, and it isn't birth control. . . . So, I require condoms, and then I would

have to be like, comfortable with the person to do like anal or anything. Um, just because I've never really done that, the [only] other person I did that with was my ex-boyfriend at the time. So I have with recurring clients. . . . I would do it [anal] with them.

In all types of sexual relationships, people can expect that their sexual boundaries will vary from partner to partner. Thus, how we articulate our desires and needs, as well as acquire informed consent, will change from person to person, context to context, and time to time.

WORKERS: WHO YOU ARE MATTERS

Based on my years of research on sex work, it is full-service providers, like Devon, from whom we learn the most about the complexities of sexual consent. Unlike many non-erotic laborers, sex workers demand the specific conditions under which they will consent to sex: there are no sheepish whispers about not preferring certain sexual behaviors or, worse, expecting the partner(s) to read nonverbal cues. Full-service providers negotiate for safer sex. Escorts, for example, will often make clear before they've even met their clients that barebacking (penetrative sex without a condom) is not permitted. Some full-service providers clearly specify that acts ranging from kissing to penetrative anal sex are not allowed or that such actions must be negotiated for additional fees.

Sex workers with marginalized identities teach us the most about the importance of clear communication when dealing with consent. They underscore the importance of individual subjectivity in discussions of consent: there is no formulaic or universal way that *all* people should navigate consent.

In my interviews with transmasculine and nonbinary escorts, it was typical for them to talk about the educational work they had to do with clients; it was a staple of their negotiations. Bailey, a white trans and gender-fluid 22-year-old escort from the United States, said, "Anytime I get a new client that doesn't know anything about like transmasculine health . . . I have to stop them and explain to them in our initial meetup because I have them meet me in a public place first, and then we discuss everything."

In some cases, clients had never had sex with a man with a vulva or a transmasculine nonbinary person with large breasts. In those cases, escorts need to use precise language when referring to parts of their body. For example, transmasculine escorts (especially those who have not had top surgery) might require that clients agree to use the term "chest," not "breasts," or the words "first and second holes" and to not use the terms "pussy," "vagina," and so forth. As Voss, a 24-year-old, white agender escort from the United States, put it, "I will like more put my foot down like, hey, this is my boundary right here. Please don't refer to me in this way. Please don't use this word. I'm not comfortable with it. And I find the majority of them are like, oh, I'm so sorry." Oliver, who is a 26-year-old, white, and Native man from the United States, told me, "I feel like escorts have the majority of the power in the situation because we're the one who is running our business. You know we don't know you. And yeah, when there are times I feel like they're starting to treat me in a way that I do not want to be like seen or treated, I'll speak up. But . . . I need to know that you're actually going to respect me and respect how I see myself, right."

As Oliver emphasizes, these negotiations are imbued with power. Exerting power and asserting one's needs are critical when acquiring consent to the sexual encounter and to feeling safe and respected. However, it is also crucial to examine how overlapping systems of oppression shape who feels entitled to or empowered to articulate their sexual needs directly.

Existing Power Arrangements Matter

Labor conditions under which sex workers perform their work shape both how they negotiate consent and the extent of their power within these negotiations. Full-service providers trading sex on the street, for example, will generally have less power in their transactions with clients than providers working in brothels or independently online. Thus, it is critically important to explore questions regarding who in the transaction feels empowered to articulate their needs, desires, and boundaries.

Sex workers have been thinking and practicing intersectionality well before it was in academic fashion. They often publicly discuss the importance of examining what they colloquially call the "whorearchy" and its product, "lateral whorephobia." The whorearchy refers to a stratification system within the sex industry that, according to Raani Begum, divides "sex workers into categories of marginally respectable to least respectable."[13] On her blog, *Street Hooker*, Graceyswer explains, "The whorearchy is used to describe the hierarchical difference between the vast number of sex workers based on the stigma they face, how intimate they are with the client and the likelihood of them having interactions with the police."[14] Queer sex worker and activist Tilly Lawless elaborates on this concept in a 2016 interview with Karley Sciortino:

> The whorearchy is the hierarchy that shouldn't—but does—exist in the sex industry, which makes some jobs within it more stigmatized than others, and some more

acceptable. Basically, it goes like this, starting from the bottom (in society's mind): street based sex worker, brothel worker, rub and tug worker/erotic masseuse, escort, stripper, porn star, BDSM mistress, cam girl, phone sex worker then finishing with sugar baby on the top.[15]

Although I have seen many diagrams outlining various hierarchies of sex work, such distinctions can thwart solidarity and reinforce lateral whorephobia.[16]

Lateral whorephobia points to how sex workers practicing privileged forms of erotic labor often look down on workers in more stigmatized sectors. Caty Simon, coeditor of "Tits and Sass," a sex-worker-run blog, described lateral whorephobia in this way in an article by Andrew Poitras for *Hopes & Fears*:

"Lateral whorephobia," which is where one kind of sex worker is maybe more privileged than another kind of sex worker, so they'll look down upon and stigmatize them, which happens so often in the community. Pro dommes will say things like, "Well, at least we don't fuck our clients" or "At least we're not whores." Porn stars will say that escorts are dirty. Escorts will say full-service pro-subs take too many risks.[17]

I had a lot of privileges as a sex worker. My wages fluctuated but were high. For the most part, my work was legal, and because even the full-service work I did was indoors, I enjoyed corporeal autonomy, freedom from police harassment, and levels of safety that many full-service sex workers do not. Although I claim the sex worker identity without reservation, the labor conditions I worked under and my experiences were privileged ones, which likely contributed to why I enjoyed much of my time doing that work.

Class, race, nationality, citizenship status, gender, and ability are all factors that contribute to how consent and its preconditions are communicated and if consent is even acquired. Dany, a 24-year-old white trans man from Belgium, underscored this point in our conversations, discussing how power dynamics shape their sexual encounters. In a discussion of barebacking, they told me,

> I have been asked for barebacking, but I don't want to do it. Also, I did it a lot when I was on Grindr. And that's something that is a social kink to me. I did a lot because the guys were insisting, or because I had smoked, or I was drunk, and I didn't think, or because of the dynamics between us, because I like being submissive, but at the same time I know very well that it's not a good thing. It's always best if you discuss it a lot. You do it with someone you know, or at least you have discussed it. But when you do hookups on Grindr you obviously don't do that. So, I knew that it was a bad idea, but I don't know, I was also looking for the adrenaline and the risk of it.

Then discussing power dynamics while working, Dany noted,

> So, the power dynamics would also affect my capacity to say no to barebacking and that happened quite a few times. But with my clients, I always do blowjobs without the condom, and . . . on a prevention website for sex workers, they would say to sex workers, never have sex without the condom. I was like, that's advice you can give to cis escorts, to cis women. But you do not use a condom if you are working with gay men. . . . But I'm trying to avoid that

[barebacking] as much as possible, and I think I would only do it if I really needed the money.

Suggesting that the answer to reducing terrible sex and sexual assault is merely better communication glosses over the existing power relationships that influence how systems shape interpersonal exchanges. As Dany noted, discussing one's needs is vital, but sexual scripts, cultural mores, stereotypes, and power relations shape the articulation of sexual needs and boundaries. Those who are especially economically vulnerable may make choices that can put themselves at risk, but such coping strategies help them navigate imbalanced power relationships.

Patriarchal gender norms and hegemonic masculinity too often muzzle women and empower men.[18] This system's entanglements with white supremacy also embolden white men and disempower others. Depending on one's position under capitalism, especially in sex industries, economic precarity can cause people to refrain from a direct discussion of their needs. I spoke with other escorts like Dany who said that there were occasions when they would agree to have sex without a condom, especially with a regular client they trusted and who paid the right price. Escorts of color might allow clients to exoticize them. An undocumented trans woman trading sex on the street may not force a client to use a condom because she needs the money, and she labors under a state that criminalizes her and denies her fundamental human rights.

Whether a person negotiates consent as a sex worker or not, consent discussions do not occur in a vacuum. I believe that straight cisgender women will continue to have terribly unsatisfying sex with cis men, even if they consent to it, because the patriarchal system has systemically disempowered them not to voice their sexual needs and desires.[19] If trans women are assaulted and even murdered in their intimate encounters with cisgender straight men, it is *not* because they failed to communicate their needs. It is because their attackers are emboldened by institutionalized cissexism and transmisogyny. Examining consent without considering the systems that shape how such conversations transpire is negligent.

Technology Is Your Friend

Many sex workers now use the internet to perform various aspects of their work. Full-service escorts use multiple communication technologies and the internet to meet, screen, and evaluate clients. James is a 34-year-old white, nonbinary bigender escort from the United States who described screening this way:

> One of the first things I do, let's say, somebody, emails me, and I asked them to text message me. I want to see if they can follow directions. Can you follow directions? You know, it's like is what I'm asking that hard, right? Like, yeah. And then when we're communicating, like, I want to see like, if they're being reciprocal, I want to see you know, Are they answering with one word? Are they answering in complete sentences? Are they reticent about offering, you know, providing me with certain information; namely, like, I'm trying to see if they're wanting me to take all the risk and they're not taking themselves. I do a number of things like this to kind of filter out D-bags [douchebags].

James reminds us that communication is critical to establishing informed consent, and actively filtering out "D-bags" promotes risk reduction, safety, and comfortability, thereby creating the context for more pleasurable encounters.

Once escorts do an initial virtual screening, many then also require a face-to-face meeting in public. Bailey, a 22-year-old trans and gender-fluid white provider from the United States, describes how this process works for them:

> So, my verification just starts off the bat with just a basic session. They email me the date and time that they want because I have a general set of availability, and it may vary, so we may have to change. How long they want the session to be. Their full name and a picture of themselves holding up their pinkie. And if they're wanting a longer session than what I advertise, I'll respond with, "Okay, then I need you to provide like a LinkedIn or a business picture of a business card for employment verification." For any kind of BDSM meetups, I require that three to five days before our session, we set up a public meetup to discuss safe words, what we're going to do. And I put in a qualifier if I am not comfortable doing a scene with you after this discussion, I can and will cancel the session because then also, if I decide to do that session with them, that's when I have them put down a down payment so if they don't show up, I'm not wasting my time.

Bailey first corresponds and screens clients via email, often asking them to verify their identity through online platforms such as LinkedIn and to send a selfie. Moreover, because full-service sex work is criminalized in most parts of the world, providers must be cautious about how much they say online, especially post-FOSTA/SESTA (Fight Online Sex Trafficking Act/Stop Enabling Sex Traffickers Act).[20] That is why Bailey then requests an in-person meeting for an explicit conversation about what services the client wants;

this is especially important for clients who want BDSM services. Note that Bailey emphasizes that they also may refuse a client if they are not comfortable with anything they've discussed. People can learn a lot about negotiating consent from kink practitioners.

The use of the internet to mediate sexual commerce keeps sex workers safer by enabling them to negotiate sexual encounters well before they happen. Their strategies can be extrapolated to those who engage in noncommercial sex. Therefore, it is vital to explore how online technologies can transform how people negotiate consent.[21] Escorts told me that they used apps such as Grindr to meet and screen clients; both providers and clients strategically use a system of emojis on the app to describe services and desires. To protect sex workers, I will not define the symbols, but Fransisco, an 18-year-old Mexican trans man from the United States, provides an example of how the emoji system on Grindr works: "I use the application Grindr. Sometimes people use emoji codes. For example, when they put [this symbol] and [this symbol, plus this symbol], that means that they also want drugs . . . and I always had to be careful with the person because I don't hang out with a person who would take drugs or alcohol [during a date]."

Many people are already using digital technologies in hookups and dating. Because of rampant racism, cissexism, and heterosexism, this is especially true for marginalized people..[22] There are now apps that can help manage consent, such as Consent Amour and Legal Fling. However, obtaining consent is not as simple as telling yourself, "Well, I've consented on the app, and we are done." Consent can be withdrawn at any time and requires ongoing discussion. However, apps can help mediate the awkwardness of conversations about consent. In an era of Grindr, Tinder, dick pics, nude selfies, and sexting, people can surely use technology as an aid to mediate these exchanges, potentially in ways that feel less awkward and create the context for less unsatisfying sex and sexual assault, and more pleasure.

Consent Is Not *Incredibly Sexy*

In popular mainstream discussions of consent, there have been constant calls to make consent hot and sexy; there are even podcasts and workshops on Eventbrite devoted to "Making Consent Sexier."[23] As Sloan writes, "Asking for consent is neither optional nor difficult. And though some people whine that direct consent-asks 'ruin the mood,' they're really just demonstrating their own lack of finesse and creativity when they say that. There are dozens of smooth, fun, and hot ways to ask for consent."[24]

These workshops miss the point: consent in and of itself is *not* generally sexy at all. The types of negotiation skills that sex workers use exemplify just how unsexy these discussions can be. It is what happens after that can be sexy and pleasurable. As a professor of Women, Gender, and Sexuality Studies, Joseph Fischel argues,

> Sex with consent is just not always sexy. Literalized as an injunction to verbally request permission for a particular sex act (*Can I place my finger in your vagina?*), "ask her first" is usually and decidedly unsexy. And the more I read the brochures, posters, and other paraphernalia of the Consent Is Sexy campaign, the more I am convinced its slogan makes little sense. People, places, things, and fantasies can be sexy; it is hard to discern how the fact of agreement to sex is the top candidate for sexiness. A blowjob with consent might be very sexy indeed, but not summarily *because* it was consensual.

A blowjob without consent is not unsexy; it is just sexual assault.[25]

Conversations regarding consent may not feel sexy at all. They can feel awkward, weird, uncomfortable, and yes, downright mood-killing, especially when they occur during sex. Thus, we may pretend that consent is always sexy or that if people could only find sexier language, it would magically lead to better sex and less sexual assault. As my section on power aimed to make clear, the only actions that can work to end sexual assault are dismantling systems such as patriarchy that empower cisgender men to rape women, cisgenderism and transmisogyny that give a license to cishet men to rape and murder trans women, and white supremacy that historically gave legal sanction to white men to rape and sexually assault Black women.

Additionally, as Fischel argues, we need better sex education and accessible and accurate information about sex. Armed with such information, talking about sex, desires, and one's sexual needs becomes more effortless. With less stigmatization of sex and more access to rigorous sex education from a young age, just like sex workers who use sexualized vernacular every day in their work, others can also develop their sexual vernacular and feel more comfortable talking about sex and consent.

In our interpersonal relationships, using more direct language and more clearly articulating our needs can create the conditions for safer, pleasurable, and sexy consensual sexual encounters. As Kellie Scott notes, "Active consent doesn't sound sexy, but it can lead to more pleasure."[26] So, *to the extent that one can*, do not worry about being sexy. Worry instead about being honest, clear, direct, assertive, and true to oneself. Feeling safe, seen, and heard creates the conditions for more pleasurable and, yes, sexier sex.

Notes

1. Jessie Patella-Rey, "Want to Figure out the Rules of Sexual Consent? Ask Sex Workers," *Washington Post*, May 21, 2018.

2. Natalie West, *We Too: Essays on Sex Work and Survival* (New York: Feminist Press, 2021); Samantha Cooney, "'They Don't Want to Include Women like Me.' Sex Workers Say They're Being Left out of the #MeToo Movement," *Time Magazine*, February 13, 2018.

3. Tarana Burke, "Me Too's Tarana Burke Says 'Make Space' for Black Survivors in New Sexual Violence Initiative," *People*, March 16, 2021; Emma Brockes, "#MeToo Founder Tarana Burke: 'You Have to Use Your Privilege to Serve Other People,'" *The Guardian*, January 15, 2018.

4. Amanda Erickson, "In 2018, #MeToo—and Its Backlash—Went Global," *Washington Post*, December 14, 2018; Anna North, "The #MeToo Movement and Its Evolution, Explained," *Vox*, October 11, 2018, https://www.vox.com/identities/2018/10/9/17933746/me-too-movement-metoo-brett-kavanaugh-weinstein; Aja Romano, "The Sexual Assault Allegations against Kevin Spacey Span Decades: Here's What We Know," *Vox*, December 24, 2018, https://www.vox.com/culture/2017/11/3/16602628/kevin-spacey-sexual-assault-allegations-house-of-cards; Megan Thomas, "Aziz Ansari Responds to Sexual Assault Allegation: 'I Was Surprised and Concerned,'" *CNN*, January 16, 2018, https://www.cnn.com/2018/01/15/entertainment/aziz-ansari-responds/index.html.

5. Laura Barcella, "After the Reckoning: #MeToo, Sex and Dating in 2018," *NBC News*, April 19, 2018, https://www.nbcnews.com/news/us-news/after-reckoning-metoo-sex-dating-2018-n867086; Brooke Knisley, "After #MeToo, College Students Wonder: What Does Consent Mean, Exactly?" *Boston Globe*, March 21, 2018.

6. Gaby Hinsliff, "Carnality and Consent: How to Navigate Sex in the Modern World," *The Guardian*, February 14, 2018.

7. Amber Amour, "35 Sexy Ways to Ask for Consent," *Huffington Post, UK,* April 28, 2016, https://www.huffingtonpost.co.uk /amber-amour/35-sexy-ways-to-ask-for-consent_b_9789458 .html.

8. Jaclyn Friedman, "Sex & Consent: It's Time to Go beyond the Rules," *Refinery29,* September 6, 2018, https://www.refinery29 .com/en-us/sex-consent-laws-yes-means-yes-jaclyn-friedman.

9. Lap-dance rooms are often open spaces with minimal privacy in which patrons can see each other. In contrast, in the champagne room, the customer has complete privacy. What happens in the champagne room varies based on the de facto rules of the individual club and the boundaries set by the dancer. Given that full-service sex work is criminalized in the United States (except for a small jurisdiction in Nevada where brothels are legal), many clubs have strict "no sex in the champagne room" policies. However, such policies generally refer to penetrative sex, and dancers can easily work around them. Given that a trip to the champagne room requires the purchase of a bottle of liquor plus paying the high hourly rate set by the dancer, clients want a special experience, even if that does not include sex. For example, the first time I ever took a customer to the champagne room, he wanted sex, and I said it was not allowed. However, after a brief negotiation, I assured him he'd cum if he was ok doing so in his pants. I danced. I mounted his lap. I gyrated. He came. We talked and drank, and if my memory serves me, I made $300 for the hour. Everyone was happy, including the club, which made money from selling the bottle and the fee it charged to enter the room.

10. Money showers, or colloquially "making it rain," is a ritual of strip club culture and refers to the fanning out of money, usually $1 bills in large amounts, over the stripper's body. In this context Roger gave the bartender a $100 bill (occasionally two), and she "showered" me in money while dancing on stage. The ritual has benefits for both the worker and client. For me, these showers

were a spectacle and thus in the context of the club raised my sexual capital; if Roger gave several money showers in one evening, it added a "bonus" to my negotiated wage for that night. For Roger, I imagine they bolstered his masculinity and sense of power in the club.

11. In sex markets, the "girlfriend experience" refers to a service in which the client wants intimacy, and not only a sexual experience. For example, in full-service markets, the client might take an escort to dinner or even on vacation, valuing time spent with the worker and not just the sex provided.

12. Born in hip-hop culture, in addition to being the title of a song by rapper E-40, the colloquialism "captain save a hoe" refers to men who try to save women whom they perceive as broken, whores, and otherwise damaged. Helping such women turn their lives around bolsters the man's self-esteem and masculinity.

13. Raani Begum, "Whorephobia and Whorearchy," *Ko-fi* (blog), March 3, 2020, https://ko-fi.com/post/Whorephobia-and -Whorearchy-V7V11H2DJ. Also see Melissa Grant, *Playing the Whore: The Work of Sex Work* (New York: Verso Books, 2014); Belle Knoxx, "Tearing down the Whorearchy from the Inside," *Jezebel*, July 2, 2014, https://jezebel.com/tearing-down-the -whorearchy-from-the-inside-1596459558; Karley Sciortino, "Sex Worker and Activist, Tilly Lawless, Explains the Whorearchy," *Slutever*, May 23, 2016, https://slutever.com/sex-worker-tilly -lawless-interview/

14. Graceyswer, "Looking up at the Whorearchy from the Bottom," April 30, 2020, https://street-hooker.com/2020/04/30/looking -up-at-the-whorearchy-from-the-bottom/ last accessed 04/22/2021.

15. Sciortino, "Tilly Lawless Explains the Whorearchy."

16. Violet Vixx, "Call Girls, Lot Lizards . . . and Every Whore in Between," October 3, 2019, *Violet Vixxx* (blog), https://www .violetprovixen.com/post/call-girls-lot-lizards-and-every-whore

-in-between. Mysterious Witt, "What Is the Whorearchy and Why It's Wrong," *An Injustice Magazine*, November 18, 2020, https://aninjusticemag.com/what-is-the-whorearchy-and-why -its-wrong-1efa654dcb22.

17. Andrew Poitras, "What Constitutes Sex Work?" *Hopes & Fears*, http://www.hopesandfears.com/hopes/now/question/216863 -what-constitutes-sex-work.

18. Angela Jones, "#DemandBetter Straight Sex!" *Bully Bloggers*, January 21, 2018, https://bullybloggers.wordpress.com/2018/01/21 /demandbetter-straight-sex-byangela-jones/.

19. Jones, "#DemandBetter Straight Sex!"

20. FOSTA was signed into law on April 11, 2018. It combined the original FOSTA bill, drafted in the House of Representatives, and the Senate's similar bill, Stop Enabling Sex Traffickers Act (SESTA). Essentially, Congress rewrote the 1996 Communications Decency Act, ending "safe harbor" protections for websites. Their concern was the exponential growth of online adult websites and their ostensible role in facilitating labor trafficking. FOSTA was a massive win for anti-porn and sex work abolitionist activists who wanted to end all sexual commerce. However, research shows FOSTA is causing deleterious transnational harms to sex workers and endangers those identified as trafficked—a fact that has been acknowledged by the U.S. Department of Justice.

21. Edward C. Baig, "Does 'Yes' Mean 'Yes?' Can You Give Consent to Have Sex to An App?" *USA TODAY*, September 26, 2018.

22. Shantel Gabrieal Buggs, "Dating in the Time of #BlackLivesMatter: Exploring Mixed-Race Women's Discourses of Race and Racism," *Sociology of Race and Ethnicity* 3, no. 4 (2017): 538–551.

23. Jasleen Singh, "Consent Is Sexy Campaign: Why Consent Is Important (and Sexy)." *Mic*, March 25, 2013, https://www.mic .com/articles/30185/consent-is-sexy-campaign-why-consent-is -important-and-sexy; Nicolas DiDomizio, "This Tumblr Post

Perfectly Demonstrates Why Consent Is Sexy." *Mic,* July 16, 2015, https://www.mic.com/articles/122424/this-tumblr-post -perfectly-demonstrates-why-consent-is-sexy; Ashani Jodha, "15 Sexperts on How to Make Consent Sexy," *Flare,* May 11, 2015, https://www.flare.com/sex-and-relationships/15-sexperts -on-how-to-make-consent-sexy/; JR Thorpe, "7 Hot Ways to Practice Affirmative Consent," *Bustle,* Feb. 11, 2016, https://www .bustle.com/articles/138297-7-ways-to-make-practicing-affirmative -consent-sexy; Kasandra Brabaw, "How to Make Consent Sexy, according to a Dominatrix." *Refinery29,* September 10, 2018, refinery29.com/en-us/bdsm-sex-consent-rules-dominatrix' Blake Zealer, "How Can You Make Consent Sexy? A Guide to Making Consent Fun and Playful without Being a Creep!" *The Good Men Project,* July 27, 2018, https://goodmenproject.com /featured-content/how-can-you-make-consent-sexy-pgtn/; Kate Orson, "When Consent Is Sexy," *Kinkly,* November 7, 2019, https://www.kinkly.com/when-consent-is-sexy/2/18345.

24. Kate Sloan, "50 Hot Ways to Ask for Consent," *Girly Juice,* November 20, 2017, https://girlyjuice.net/50-hot-ways-ask -consent/.

25. Joseph Fischel, *Screw Consent: A Better Politics of Sexual Justice* (Oakland: University of California Press, 2019), 12.

26. Kellie Scott, "Active Consent Doesn't Sound Sexy, but It Can Lead to More Pleasure," *ABC Everyday*, October 27, 2019, https://www.abc.net.au/everyday/active-consent-can-lead-to -more-pleasure/11473678.

2

Consent in the Dark

ALEXANDER CHEVES

Consent beyond Boundaries

There are lovely men in the world who like to get fucked up the ass by hands and arms. I'm one of them. In the United States, we call this "fisting," while our neighbors in Europe say "handballing." As a fetish practice, fisting first gained popularity (and notoriety) in gay leather culture during the 1970s and 1980s.

Most experienced fisters will at some point take two fists, which is called double-fisting, or doubles. When I took mine, I told my fisting friends—"FFriends"—all about it. They congratulated me as one might congratulate someone for putting a down payment on a house: "You did it!" "Way to go!" "I remember my first time!"

But one friend asked, "Did you ask him to do it?"

The truth is that I did not. In fact, I told him to slow down, a request he mostly ignored. In the minutes leading up to the moment when I took two, I actually asked him to stop and said that I needed a break.

He growled, "No, you're ready." And he was right—I was. I did. And when I did, I floated on a cloud of euphoria for the rest of the night.

At the start of the session, he was gentle. He said, "I'm not going to hurt you." And he didn't. This was not our first time playing together, and based on our past sex nights, I trusted him. He knew what he was doing. He knew when to push my limits, when to listen to my "no," and when to charge past it. Not every fister would agree that these attributes make a good top—everyone likes different things. I enjoyed him, and my nights with him felt like many nights I had enjoyed with other tops, men who used a degree of dominance and degradation in their play, men who expanded my boundaries and expanded my hole.

Some would call this "consensual kink." I would. I just didn't fully consent to his speed, to the stretch, at that particular moment, in that small part of the night. I wanted the rest, but afterward, I was grateful for all of it. No, I didn't ask him to double-fist me. I didn't even particularly want him to. I gave him every indication that he should stop. So, was this assault?

I don't believe it was, mainly because I didn't feel assaulted. Quite the opposite: after we played, I was proud of myself and thankful that he knew when not to listen. I was grateful that it didn't go the other way—that I didn't get hurt or feel scared.

Fisting, at least for me, is one of those rare spaces where the established rules of consent sometimes get murky—where I might not fully know what I want while someone else might have a clearer idea of my desires. This might challenge some people's notion of sexual autonomy, and I understand that might be frightening or even angering, but this is my experience from the sex I love. The work of getting fisted requires one to step away from the mind's natural defenses, the body's resistance and tension, and literally open oneself up to whatever comes, to whatever is being dealt. When you get to that place, then fisting gets good.

In fisting, sometimes my "no" means "stop." Other times, with certain playmates, my "no" can be overridden, and I accept this. Inversely, sometimes I say "yes" when my body says "no"—this happens when there's tension in my muscles and mind that I can't let go of, which keeps me from fully surrendering. The body nearly always wins, even when I'm begging for it.

Overriding that "no" is not always without consequence—but no part of fisting is. This is a high-risk sex sport. The physical risks of harm and injury are substantial, no matter how hard or gently a person likes to play. Most of us know someone who went too rough and ended up in the Emergency Room.

When my "yes" and "no" are not always clear to me, how can they be clear to him? How can anyone be expected to read my words, my breathing, my face, which over a single session may feel and say many different things? In kink, we have "safe words," which when said require sex (or whatever else is happening) to stop immediately. These words are useful for role-playing scenarios in which saying "no" might be part of the fantasy, and I use them. But safe words, although useful in many kink scenes, rely on the assumption that people are always able to discern what they want in an intense moment—that they are not susceptible then to pressures (internal or external), persuasion, comforting, coaxing, and their own ambition. Safe words don't necessarily make extreme sex safer, and they certainly can't prevent people from feeling assaulted after the fact.

I don't know why fisting is so beautiful, but I do know it still scares me sometimes. It challenges my assumptions of consent; more than that, it reminds me—as someone devoted to doing it—how my body and health often hang in the balance of complex nonverbal communication, how my safety is literally in the hands of someone else.

Long before I discovered fisting, I learned—or perhaps was taught—to be comfortable with sexual situations like this by pursuing other kinds of sex I like. As do many other queer men who occupy a certain subset of gay life, I enjoy high-risk sex with multiple partners (anonymous sex, backroom sex, sex with strangers in video stores, and in the shadowy corners of dance clubs). I tend to get more sexually transmitted infections than those who use condoms or who only have sex with one person at a time. Sometimes guys like us call ourselves "pigs."

When asked about my sex life at the clinic, I struggle to provide estimates of how many sex partners I've had in the last six months—and the twelve-month question I don't even bother with because I have no idea of the answer. It's odd to me that we still ask people these questions in a clinical setting. But in these moments, I am reminded that the average heterosexual person must have fewer sex partners than I do; perhaps even the average queer man does too. I know that I differ from many people, queer and otherwise, by not ascribing any deeper meaning to sex beyond physical pleasure. I don't entertain any purity myths, and I don't believe in the concept of sin. I see group sex as a fun weekend activity that's better than a movie but requires a bit more preparation.

Most of my sex partners are cisgender men like me, and cis-maleness brings with it social privileges that allow us to live as hedonistically as we do. Cis-maleness is not the only privilege I benefit from. I am white and come from a well-to-do family, so my perspective of the medical system is skewed as a result: I've never struggled to find health insurance, never distrusted doctors or medicine, and always found treatment when I needed it. Most of the cis gay men I know who enjoy similar sex lives to mine have access to competent health care. Many take PrEP, a daily pill that prevents HIV, which can be unaffordable for people without good insurance. The ones not taking PrEP are often like me—HIV-positive and taking medication (most of these men in my immediate and tangential sexual orbits live in places in the United States and Europe where such HIV medications are available). And many—but, notably, not all—of us are comfortable with versions of consent that have become controversial in the wake of #MeToo: "situational consent" and "assumed consent." Both of these essentially state that, in a sexual environment, if someone doesn't protest, then they want it.

Consent, like all concepts, is an invention of language. It assumes a stark distinction between "yes" and "no," and for it to work and for people to be safe, we must believe in this distinction, even though it might get murky in real sex—especially hardcore and "nontraditional" sex.

Is there an argument for a person's unspoken doubts and hesitations qualifying as a verified "no"? Can these feelings become, on reflection, a verified "no" after the fact and make a consensual encounter later feel like a nonconsensual one? And if so, can those feelings ever be enough to incriminate someone? I don't think so—and I am afraid of the people who answer those questions affirmatively. The dangerous people in our midst whom we don't talk about enough are the ones eager to pathologize and outlaw the forms of sex they do not understand and therefore cannot allow to exist.

Consent in the Dark

Dark rooms and backrooms count as the best parts of my sex life. These are lights-out sex spaces that can be found in gay establishments (bars, clubs) across the world. They are sometimes intentionally set up by the owners or formed "by the people"—randy patrons eager to fuck each other—making them beautifully egalitarian, democratic, and rogue. They are relics, at least in the United States, of an antiquated gay male ethos that once existed outside the law and away from the media spotlight.

After enough experiences in backrooms, each one begins to feel familiar—like a small- town gay bar. It's not so much their physicality as a space that becomes comfortable and recognizable because their dimensions, features, and degrees of shadowiness vary. What makes them feel familiar are the unspoken rules of engagement that exist within them, which feel like a near-universal language of cruising, touching, and groping freely. In the right space, queer men who speak in different tongues all miraculously know how to unbuckle their pants, touch, drop to their knees, and bend over. In the dark, the rules of consent change. The verbal cues of the outside world become foreign. Hands grope. A rejection comes not in the form of a "no" but instead of a silent headshake or by simply shuffling away.

In short, consent in these spaces is practiced differently than in the outside world. This became painfully obvious to me in the wake of an incident at one of my favorite spots in the South. In 2017, a straight woman wandered behind the black curtain and into the backroom of a gay bar in Atlanta. When someone touched her, she threatened to call the police. Fearing a police raid and shutdown (something queer people are very familiar with), the gay owners of the bar installed bright lights, took down the curtain, and turned the backroom into a smoking lounge.

I assumed the closure would be permanent. Who wouldn't? Backrooms have been vanishing since the 1980s and the advent of AIDS. Most cities and even small towns in the United States once had one or several such spaces.

Today, they are relatively rare. Their decline can be partially credited to the broader decline in the number of gay establishments. To survive, gay bars have had to clean up and make their spaces and events more palatable to a new kind of clientele: straight women screaming "Yaaas!" in matching bachelorette dresses. Ironically, straight women often now outnumber the queer patrons at gay bars across America.

Today, most gay bars in New York—the city made legendary for its cruisy docks and shipping containers down the West Side—do not have a backroom. In SoMa, San Francisco's notorious leather neighborhood, the backroom of a widely loved, distinctly slutty leather bar was destroyed some years ago when an incident similar to the one in Atlanta occurred: someone who was not a queer man walked in and felt assaulted, not understanding how these spaces work for us. Stories like this have been happening across the country, and in the wake of #MeToo, these spaces seem all the more endangered.

When a person walks into a backroom, they waive a degree of consent. Queer men like to go in them to get groped and touched. That's why these spaces exist.

Most socially cognizant queer men would never touch a stranger without their consent in any other public place. But in a dark room, doing that is not just tolerable but also expected. It is sometimes jarring to step into a place where, under the cover of anonymity afforded by darkness and an unspoken agreement to keep chatter to a minimum, the rules of human engagement shift. But they do, and those who don't feel comfortable in these spaces—as even many queer men do not—simply stay away.

There's no great schism between these camps of queer men. For generations, we have peacefully lived and let live. Queer men who don't like anonymous sex or being touched by strangers just stay by the bar or on the dance floor and don't worry about the queer men who wander to the back. We peacefully coexist.

Worshipping Consent

I think most people like to think of consent as a fixed thing, something that exists without nuance or interpretation, especially now in the wake of #MeToo. And maybe this is just because I'm very kinky, but I don't see it that way at all. I think consent is incredibly nuanced, contingent on two or more people's interpretation and interaction at that time and place. In hardcore kink and BDSM, dialogue establishes the rules of consent for each individual session: consent, for us, is the most customizable thing in the world.

For this reason, I'm against efforts to standardize "enthusiastic consent," especially in law. Enthusiastic consent is generally considered a "Hell yes!"—a direct, verbal affirmation before and continuously during a sexual encounter asserting that a person wants whatever is being done.

I understand the need for this model of consent, which is often described as a better alternative to the "no means no" model. Many people—particularly women—are taught not to say "no," to be nice, to spare men's feelings and fears of rejection. In some situations, many people might not entirely know how to say "no" or may not even feel safe saying "no." Alcohol and other substances can make matters even more complicated.

Enthusiastic consent attempts to accommodate for the failings of past consent models by requiring people to communicate and agree not just to a sexual encounter but also to every stage of it, just as a person might consent to one sexual activity over the course of an encounter but not another.

In an article for *The Swaddle*, writer Pallavi Prasad explains how enthusiastic consent might look in practice:

This constant conversation about what the two people want to do to each other and have done to themselves needs to take place before and during sex. Whoever said sex doesn't need to be talked about, didn't know what he was saying. Great sex requires great communication. Becoming comfortable enough to have these conversations may take time, especially if it's a new concept, but it is nothing regular practice can't solve. A few ways to seek enthusiastic consent could be asking, "Hey, I would love to do _____ with you. May I?" "You know what I really want to do in bed? _____. How does that sound to you?" and/or "Is it okay if I _____?" It is also important to learn how to articulate the denial of enthusiastic consent, which can be as simple as "I'm not really into what we're doing right now; can we just stick to _____?" "I'm not in the mood for this" or "That's not something I feel comfortable doing, but I'll let you know if that changes."[1]

As a queer man, this reads to me as an incredibly heteronormative—and incredibly unsexy—description of sex. It assumes (a) that sex involves just two people; (b) that these people are at home or in some private place where they can have this dialogue; (c) that the lights are on and they can see each other; and (d) that these people are able and willing to have a conversation. Most of my sex life looks nothing like that, and I don't want it to.

I like getting a little fucked up, losing my inhibitions, and fucking strangers I don't know or care about—and there are many people out there, queer and otherwise, just like me. The queer men of my tribe may hesitate to say this too loudly, but for many of us, "enthusiastic consent" is alien to our sex lives. One of my great loves, a man in New York, mirrors my interests and desires, and we push each other to try new things. He once confessed that when he was younger, he took drugs with sleeping pills to fuck himself up so badly that he could not physically object to sex, and in this state, he invited guys over to do whatever they wanted. I've done similar things.

Losing control is erotic (and, as we're aware, dangerous). More pointedly, he and I have almost certainly fucked men— at sex parties and elsewhere—who were too high to object. But just like the proverbial backroom, by being in those spaces, they waived a degree of consent. Situationally, bent over, ass up, hungry, they wanted it.

Queer people (of all ages and genders) have ample experience being outlawed. We're no strangers to straight definitions of proper sexual behavior branding us as social miscreants. And as an HIV-positive man, I'm sensitive to how well-meaning laws passed by straights can result in the criminalization of innocent people. States with HIV criminalization laws continue to put people living with a disease in prison, simply because they have an illness the world does not understand.

I don't have an alternative model of consent to propose, and those who promise easy answers to such complex questions should not be trusted. I can't end this by proposing an ideal model of consent that will work for all communities across the globe. But I am saying that "enthusiastic consent" will not work for us all. Its proponents mean well, but this model simply will not work in the sex cultures that I and countless others call home.

I say this as someone who knows firsthand the harms and risks that can accompany sex. I have been assaulted before. I have also been in situations where I was touched by people who didn't ask first (or say anything to me first). These are two different experiences.

The #MeToo movement is a response to rapists, men in power who manipulate and coerce women in the workplace and elsewhere. It calls out the industries that normalize and protect this behavior. It reveals, in my mind, a clear and obvious wrong, one that stretches back through human history. If pressed, I would probably admit that righting the wrong of systemic violence against women is more important than protecting the sex cultures I cherish. But I do not think these two projects are mutually exclusive.

I picture the women who've come forward in the movement to tell their stories, and I wonder what they might say to me. I imagine they would tell me that women have been demanding justice for longer than gay men like me have been fucking in orgiastic pits. But queer men are not the enemy here. I'll state it directly: there's something wrong with straight men, and queer men have always known this. We've been beaten and bullied by them for generations. We know how dangerous they can be. The problem of them isn't remedied by policing us.

On my first visit to San Francisco several years ago, I went to a gay sex club. I was very nervous—I had tested HIV-positive just a few months earlier. I walked through the dense rooms where guys were fucking, one on one or in little groups, without any words passed between them. I watched and learned. I wanted to join in, but I didn't know how to disclose my HIV status. Doing so would require a conversation, which appeared to be inappropriate in the space. I eventually found myself standing under a red EXIT sign when a man walked up wearing a leather vest. Even in the dim light, I saw he had blue eyes. Without a word, he started touching me, and I said, "Hey, I just have to say this: I'm HIV-positive."

He looked at me and said, "I don't give a fuck about your status," then pushed me over and fucked me over a bench.

Before him, I felt untouchable and believed my HIV was a hideous thing I had to carry around and reveal within a heavy and difficult conversation. He was my first taste of bareback culture, my first evidence that some queer men don't give a fuck—they're just here to fuck.

Men in bareback culture assume all the risks by being in these places. These risks include the possibility of being touched (and more) by someone they don't find attractive—by someone too aggressive, too fucked up to notice a lack of interest, and these situations do happen. But by being there, they are choosing—consenting—to navigate this field and play in this realm. And I always leave these places feeling a distinct love for my own people that I can hardly put into words.

I know some people would have watched my interaction with the blue-eyed man and called it rape, but I could kiss his feet. I've heard people call my sex "problematic"—even other queer men have told me that it "pushes a line" and "propagates rape culture." But in my life, at least, it saved me in every way. If I have to be a criminal to enjoy it, so be it.

Note

1. Pallavi Prasad, "Consent Is More than just a Yes to Sex, It's an Enthusiastic Yes," *Swaddle*, September 17, 2019, https://theswaddle .com/enthusiastic-consent/.

3

Lost in the Dark—Or How I Learned to Queer Consent

TREVOR HOPPE

A mentor of mine came of age in the 1960s when "homo-sexual" was still the right word for it. He was in college when he first fooled around with another guy. Neither of them had a clue what they were supposed to do, but . . . his friend had heard that gay sex had *something* to do with Vaseline. And, so, they decided to smear each other with it and see what happened. I still laugh imagining them writhing around in the slippery paste for hours, bewildered, lost in the dark, but nonetheless pretty turned on.

This chapter is inspired by his story as I reflect on my own. How do you say "yes" to sex when you aren't exactly sure what you want? How do you say "no" when a boundary is crossed, and you need a situation to end? Despite having internet access since the moment I hit puberty, I have also spent much of my sexual life lost in the dark.

Part of figuring out what turns you on is necessarily also about figuring out what consent means in practice. Is it just the absence of a "no"? In recent years, some feminists have pushed back against that idea. They argue that this passive concept of consent ignores the many reasons people are unable to say no. Consent, they argue, ought to be thought of instead as actively given to partners in an *enthusiastic* manner—or, what one Australian university resource describes as "a continuous state of being between people that actively affirms their wishes. It is checking in with the other person, every step of the way."[1] This notion of checking in is sometimes framed as repeated permission-seeking for each sexual act: "This concept requires that consent be given to each piece of sexual activity."[2]

I admit that enthusiastic consent may be useful for sex ed. Education requires setting aspirational goals for students to strive toward in their lives. We teach teenagers in driver's ed to follow the speed limit and to always keep their hands on the steering wheel at 9 and 3. But let's face it: every driver's ed teacher knows that most (if not all) of their students will wind up speeding and occasionally driving with their knees. Enthusiastic consent could be a similarly useful teaching tool for young people in the throes of learning about sex for the first time.

Useful for education, sure—but as a yardstick for assessing harm, it is not: it is just too disconnected from reality. To say that any sexual encounter that diverges from the "enthusiastic" model is necessarily assaultive or unethical would mean labeling nearly all the sex ever had in the world as assault. And if everything is assault, then nothing is. That's not just silly: it does real harm by demeaning the lived experiences of sexual assault survivors.

In this chapter, I reflect on what I learned about consent from my experiences as a gay man. Based on those experiences, there are at least three reasons that consent in the real world does not much resemble the kind described by proponents of enthusiastic consent:

1. Consent is often *nonverbal*. In my experience, consent is almost always achieved more subtly: a sigh, a moan, a pleading, a slight nudge away or toward a body part. Please don't stop doing what you're doing to ask me whether that feels good. You *know* it does based on the way I'm arching my back and moaning.

2. Consent can be *prearranged*, hashed out before you're even in the same room. For many gay men like me who hook up online, part of how we practice consent is by sexting about what gets us off before we even think to drop a pin. I don't need to ask you if you like your feet massaged. Your profile name was just a combination of the word "foot" with a bunch of massage emojis. I already know.

3. Consent can be, well, *unenthusiastic*. Ask anyone in a long-term relationship. When my husband spoons me in the morning, I might turn around and think to myself, "God, I hate morning breath." But you know what? I kiss him. Because that's how relationships work.

Enthusiastic consent may be a good teaching tool, but we need to think in more complex ways about how consent works in practice. I think queer communities, including gay men, have a special expertise that can greatly enrich our conversations about consent in this #MeToo moment. We invented and perfected many radical and public sex cultures that often involve doing consent in silence or even in the dark—in the dimly lit bathhouse, the woodsy area of the local park, the backroom of a gay bar with bass thumping so loud you can't hear your own thoughts.

In this chapter, I offer my insights based on several decades of having sex—including sometimes disappointing, frustrating, or downright bad sex. Although I am trained as a sociologist of sexuality, I do not offer scientific knowledge per se in this chapter but rather insights gleaned through my experiences.

I acknowledge at the outset that my stories and reflections are precisely that—my own. I am a white, cisgendered gay man born in the 1980s whose first sexual experiences were facilitated by a computer my dad bought the family in the mid-1990s. It was an expensive computer. I never cruised for sex—the closest I came to that was giving a blowjob to my high school friend across the cul-de-sac when I was 14. My sexual career began early and, I'm happy to say, remains a rich source of inspiration more than twenty years later.

After all that sex, this is what I've learned.

Learning to Say Yes...

How are you supposed to figure out what turns you on? What you want someone to do to—or with—you? As a queer person, what I wanted sexually was not obvious, and figuring that out was not easy. Nobody taught me about it in school. I never saw gay sex in mainstream movies. What you cannot learn from books takes practice—*practice, practice, practice.*

For me, the possibility of having sex as a young person was tantalizing—the taboo mixed with raging hormones was a heady combination. I started having gay sex as a teenager in the 1990s in North Carolina, when any sexual act with another man was still classified under the law as a felony.

I would arrange clandestine meetings with men I met online. Driving to their house, it felt like my heart was beating one thousand times a minute. What would they look like? Would they be a good kisser? Do I even *want* to kiss them?

As a horny teen, I'd usually try to make the most of any situation. This was long before smartphones. To have a picture online, you would need to have a physical photo scanned and uploaded. Webcams were invented somewhere along the way but weren't common for some time. In other words, you were often in for a surprise when they opened the door.

I spent my teenage and college years having a lot of sex with strangers. In those early years, I mostly kind of went along with anything—well, anything within reason. I didn't really understand yet whether I was a "top" or a "bottom" (or neither). If a guy asked whether I liked a certain thing done or in a certain way, what was I going to say? "Sure! I mean . . . I guess I could get into armpits?" (cue the *Arrested Development* narrator explaining that I would later find out that I was not, in fact, into them).

These formative years are critical to understanding one's erotic self. During the 1990s and 2000s when I started learning to have sex, Craigslist was a popular tool for seeking it out. Though many may think of it today as sketchy or weird, I *loved* Craigslist. The temporary, ephemeral nature of their classifieds-like ad system allowed you to try on a fantasy for an afternoon or an evening (as compared to Grindr and Scruff today that use static profiles featuring face or body pictures that rarely change). On Craigslist, you would post an anonymous ad to "Men Seeking Men" that explained what you were looking for and when. Men would respond via email. And if you were lucky, you found a match.

In addition to being a tool for meeting up, Craigslist also provided great reading material to a young person. You got to see what other people were looking for—what they found hot. When I interviewed bottom-identified gay men for a research project some years ago, I remember one of the participants was so proud of his Craigslist ads.[3] He claimed to be the first guy in San Francisco to post an ad looking for a blindfolded, "cumdump" encounter—basically a scene where you invite guys over, get on your bed blindfolded with your face down and ass in the air, and let anyone invited enter your home, fuck you without a condom, cum in you, and leave. He bragged to me that other guys would copy and paste his exact ad language into their own postings, a kind of fantasy replication made possible through this anonymous message board.

Beyond just a tool for exploring new sexual possibilities you didn't know you were into, Craigslist also taught me the value of hashing out ahead of time exactly what I wanted to happen. Although descriptions of sex in the enthusiastic consent literature make it sound like there will be a lot of talking during sex about what you like or don't, I find that this is almost never the case. Indeed, in the "cumdump" scene just described, part of what makes it hot is precisely the *lack* of dialogue—the objectification of the bottom in service of the top's physical pleasures (or so goes the sexual fantasy; obviously, there is pleasure in it for both parties).

The internet is a gift for people everywhere for this reason. Although Craigslist has been forced to shut down its personals section because of a terrible anti-sex federal law, smartphone apps facilitate similar (albeit less anonymous) ends.[4] You need only send a potential partner a few XXX messages describing a particular desire or fantasy and see how they respond. If, after a few exchanges, you manage to keep turning each other on, it is probably worth arranging a meet-up.

This is one key difference between the heterosexual #MeToo consent discourse and my experiences as a gay man. I can count on one hand the number of times I had sex with someone I did not first meet online. It is extraordinarily rare.

Research suggests that my online habits are typical for a queer person. According to a 2019 Pew Research study, more than 55% of lesbian, gay, and bisexual survey respondents reported using online apps to meet partners, versus only 28%

of straight respondents.[5] I suspect the rate is even higher for just gay men.

Of course, a few sexy chat exchanges ahead of time is not always enough. Sex also involves communication in the moment to help your partner understand what you want and what you do not enjoy. But this again reveals a limitation of the enthusiastic consent concept: this communication is often or sometimes even exclusively nonverbal: a moan, a nudge, or even a notable silence can go far.

Sexual communication is a skill. And like any skill, it must be learned and honed over time. Is he doing something that you don't really enjoy? Here's how to communicate that you're not really into that without ruining the moment (e.g., gently guiding his hand, mouth, body away from one place and toward another). Is he being too aggressive? Here's how to get him to take it easy (simply shifting weight and asking for a minute to breathe can work). And, in rare cases, is he continuing to do something that I've expressly told him not to do? Here's how to get him off you ("STOP" or, if need be, try to shove him off you and exit the situation).

…And No

I have only had to force a guy off me one time. I was living in San Francisco while going to graduate school. I met up with this very handsome man who lived a few blocks away. The encounter began simply enough, with the usual ritual of making out while slowly stumble-walking backward toward the bedroom. Then we started having sex, but I wasn't ready. It hurt. And I told him to stop and tried to pull away.

He misunderstood me—I imagine that he thought that I was acting out a rape fantasy bit. He whispered, "Oh no you don't" and pushed me down. I'm not sure what I said to him, but I do remember that I turned around and shoved him with all my might to get him off me. He was instantly apologetic and embarrassed. I got dressed immediately and left. We never spoke again.

I left his apartment feeling deeply conflicted. I truly don't believe that he was trying to assault me. But I do think he took things too far without laying the necessary groundwork, either in advance or in the moment.

I share this story knowing full well that not everyone is physically able to shove a partner around in the bedroom. He was much stronger than me, but I guess adrenaline helped. I will never know for sure, but I suspect yelling "Stop" would have achieved similar ends.

I often compare this sex-fail to an encounter I had years later while visiting Philadelphia. I think I met the guy on a website called Manhunt. His apartment was so dark that I can barely remember his face. But I do remember that our bodies just *clicked*. Everything just felt right. He was assertive and verbal *and* a great kisser. As the encounter played out, however, he got increasingly assertive and dominant—much more so than anything we had discussed ahead of time. It began to border on a rape scene. But I can still remember him stopping and looking me in the eye at each juncture, silently searching my eyes, as if to say, "Is this OK?" I would try to signal "yes" with a slight nod. It seemed that, for both of us, words would have ruptured the domination fantasy playing out before our eyes.

The great irony is—in that moment—despite theatrically performing a total lack of control and utter submission, I felt like I was fully in the driver's seat. It took me more than a decade of sexual practice to get to a point where I felt comfortable in that kind of a situation. To trust myself and to trust a stranger to let that scene play out. I felt, based on prior experience, that I could find a way to stop him if that trust broke down at any point. I trusted myself enough to let him push me far beyond my normal boundaries. In the end, it was one of the most exhilarating and erotic sexual encounters of my life.

Lost in the Dark

I often think about what it means that one of the hottest encounters in my life was basically a rape scene.

I know that sentence is heavy—believe me, the feeling is mutual. Rape is a crime. Rape is violence. But as a sexual fantasy, it represents an utter lack of control. And that fantasy is not rare: a recent review of research suggests that between 31% and 57% of women have fantasies about non-consensual sex.[6] Although I could not locate similar estimates for LGBT populations, the prevalence of gay male gangbang prisoner/prison guard rape pornography suggests they may be similarly high.

I admit that this kind of scene stretches many peoples' ideas of what consent ought to look like in practice. That kind of power play makes many people uncomfortable. But the truth is that sex is always about power. We cannot wish that away.[7] Although not for everyone, the feeling of dominating someone or of being subjugated can be exhilarating or even cathartic.[8]

Whatever the scene, the underlying fundamentals of consent remain the same. In this case, I knew from our discussions beforehand that he wanted to be in control. I told him that I wanted that—that I wanted to be an object for his pleasure. At many times throughout the encounter, he stopped what he was doing, looked directly in my eyes, and checked in with me.

Admittedly, what played out was much more forceful and aggressive than I expected. But a foundation of trust remained intact throughout, made possible by subtle but present forms of communication and checking-in.

In an ideal world, we would have had a more formal discussion about what we were going to do and what our boundaries were in advance. But I was not an experienced SM practitioner (I'm still not). And I suspect he was learning too. Like so many of us, I was exploring the realms of my own desires in the moment.

Most of us do not go into every encounter as erudite scholars of our own libidos. Even with age and practice, we can still manage to be surprised by what can turn us on in the right context, with the right partner. It is not practical to expect everyone to be able to speak these sometimes unknown desires verbally, frankly, explicitly.

We are so often lost in the dark.

A practical concept of consent must be capacious enough to allow for this kind of boundary pushing and spontaneity for those who seek it—while, of course, respecting harder lines for those who need them.

This does not mean that partners should have license to do whatever they want. Checking in, even subtly, is part of sexual communication. Unless they asked you to act this way, bulldozing over a partner's signals, and disrespecting their wishes, is at the very minimum rude. And yes, it can become assaultive behavior.

As someone who has historically been more of a bottom in my community, I've dealt with my share of bulldozing tops. Guys sometimes seem downright oblivious to their bottom partner's desires and their physical limits. Sometimes pushing at those boundaries can be hot, as I've already described. But there's a necessary feedback loop that must happen to keep consent and trust in place. It doesn't have to be a Vaseline-lens softcore "Is this ok?" moment, slow-kissing down someone's body. The occasional thrust followed by a

"You like that, boy?" is a mightily useful expression for tops that simultaneously checks in *and* feeds the erotic charge of the moment.

We must find ways to promote consent that nonetheless allow space for those of us who like to get lost in the dark. Blindly feeling around and searching—that's when I find I learn the most about myself and my desires. More than two decades and several hundred sexual encounters later, I still manage to surprise myself when I stumble on a yet-unexplored nook or cranny in my erotic mind. Here's to another two decades of exploring—and, who knows, perhaps a few more hundred encounters.

Notes

1. UNE Life, "How to Ask for Enthusiastic Consent," December 27, 2019, https://www.unelife.com.au/blog/2019/12/27/how-to-ask-for-enthusiastic-consent.

2. Elfity, "Why Do People Hate the Concept of Enthusiastic Consent?" *Persephone Magazine*, May 4, 2012, https://persephonemagazine.com/2012/05/why-do-people-hate-the-concept-of-enthusiastic-consent/.

3. See Brian's narrative in Trevor Hoppe, "Circuits of Power, Circuits of Pleasure: Sexual Scripting in Gay Men's Bottom Narratives," 14, no. 2 (2011): 205.

4. For a discussion of how FOSTA-SESTA killed Craigslist personal ads, see Aja Romano, "A New Law Intended to Curb Sex Trafficking Threatens the Future of the Internet as We Know It," *Vox*, July 2, 2018, https://www.vox.com/culture/2018/4/13/17172762/fosta-sesta-backpage-230-internet-freedom.

5. Monica Anderson, Emily A. Vogels, and Erica Turner, "The Virtues and Downsides of Online Dating," *Pew Research Center*, February 6, 2020, https://www.pewresearch.org/internet/2020/02/06/the-virtues-and-downsides-of-online-dating/.

6. Joseph W. Critelli and Jenny M. Bivona, "Women's Erotic Rape Fantasies: An Evaluation of Theory and Research," *Journal of Sex Research*, 45, no. 1 (2008): 57–70.

7. I doubt there is such a thing as egalitarian sex. There are plenty of forms of difference that divide us—by race, by class status, by age. Among gay men, gendered perceptions of masculinity still manage to divide the "twink" and the "bear." In my experience, sexual partners are never truly on an equal footing.

8. A recent study highlighted the ways in which consensual BDSM experiences can be productively exploratory for people. See Emma L. Turley, "'Like Nothing I've Ever Felt Before': Understanding Consensual BDSM as Embodied Experience." *Psychology & Sexuality*, 7, no. 2 (2016): 149–162.

4

The Straight Rules Don't Apply

Lesbian Sexual Ethics

JANE WARD

Heteropatriarchy ruins everything about straight sex—in my view anyway. It makes being a girl a mortification. It makes power a misogynistic minefield. It takes delicious perversions like BDSM and often drains them of their disruptive potential, offering only a slight variation on the tired theme of women's submission and men's dominance. It reduces many of my feminist aspirations—my greatest hopes for straight people, in particular—to something as unexciting and simplistic as sexual *equity*. Despite my devotion to queer sex practices that complicate things and make sex feel confusing, weird, or even scary, I concede that straight sex—already plagued by men's entitlement, coercion, and violence—arguably would benefit from less time spent playing around in the erotic gray areas and fulfilling all of Daddy's needs, and more time following some strict feminist rules and regulations. When you're fucking in the shadow of misogyny, mainstream feminism's modest recommendation that good sex is defined by the presence of reciprocity and enthusiastic consent makes perfect sense.

Underlying the concept of consent is an understanding that sexual equity and reciprocity are vital correctives to men's sexual entitlement and self-centeredness. This belief, one that I share, emerges from straight women's lived experiences struggling for pleasure and agency under the erotically lopsided conditions of patriarchy.[1] One of the key insights that emerged from feminist commentary about the #MeToo movement is that a flabbergasting number of straight women, in addition to surviving sexual assault and coercion, have *consented* to bad, male-centric, one-sided sex. For Black, Indigenous, and other women of color, the gap between heterosexuality's false promise of fulfillment and the realities of heteropatriarchy is widened by the expectation that straightness is one form of privilege available to women of color.[2] Patriarchy ensures that heterosexuality is itself a "rigged game" that normalizes men's sexual entitlement, prioritizes men's pleasure, and relegates sex acts that produce women's orgasms—like oral sex—to the realm of the optional.[3] As feminist blogger Reina Gattuso has argued, this kind of pleasureless (for women) straight sex—organized around women's service to men—hardly registers as bad sex at all: "It's normal sex. Normal, boring, vaguely dehumanizing hetero sex. Which is precisely the point: The normalcy."[4] Under conditions of patriarchy, laborious and unwanted sex is not the same thing as sexual assault because straight women habitually *consent* to this kind of sex (especially with husbands and boyfriends) to keep the peace, even when they are not "in the mood."[5] Patriarchy is not only a system that gives men power over women but one that also compels women to participate in normalizing—not to mention, romanticizing and eroticizing—the very system that decenters their own satisfaction.

Hence, consent is a necessary but insufficient ingredient in the making of nonviolent or non-oppressive sex. Consent must not merely be present but also *enthusiastic* in its expression—with this enthusiasm designed to measure not just what women are willing to do but also what they are hungry and eager to do. As Maggie Nelson puts it, "The #MeToo era at times seems to suggest that the principal way out of heterosexual malaise is role reversal—that [straight] women should feel emboldened to make first moves, rather than waiting for men to be the active party."[6] In all practicality, straight girls and women might be hungry and eager for many kinds of sex, including the same old sex acts that have left women notoriously orgasm-less (giving men blowjobs, getting fucked without clitoral stimulation). But implicit in the discourse about enthusiastic consent is the presumption that it will encourage sexual egalitarianism or a reciprocal distribution of pleasure in which women's sexual needs are attended to "equally" with those of men.

Sexual Egalitarianism or Not

For lesbians, sexual mutuality and equity is hardly a new idea. Second-wave lesbian feminism heralded sexual egalitarianism "as an antidote to patriarchal sexual domination of women" and understood sex as a kind of "turn taking" of erotic labors in which each participant received only as much pleasure as they gave.[7] According to Laura Harris, this prescription helped animate "cultural notions of lesbian sex as laboriously egalitarian," exemplified by iconic television scenes in which straight women (such as Samantha on *Sex and the City* or Grace in *Will and Grace*) explain that they can't be lesbians because it involves "too much extra work."[8]

And yet, nonegalitarian sex remains a mainstay of lesbian erotic culture; truth be told, the possibility that many of us are (or wish to be) bottoms who revel in our pleasure without concern for the other is something of a running joke in lesbian spaces. This is where the egalitarianism implicit in straight feminist articulations of enthusiastic consent reveal their heteronormative underpinnings. Sexual selfishness and sexual service mean something altogether different outside of heteropatriarchal sex. For instance, Laura Harris offers the "pillow queen" (or the pillow princess) as a figure of anti-capitalist transgression: her "sexual laziness, her refusal to equate sex with labor, may be read as a self-pleasuring resistance to capitalist imperatives of gendered sexual labor."[9] Harris argues that queers should celebrate the pillow queen—typically a femme figure—who lies on her pillow "receiving pleasure, demanding pleasure, luxuriating in pleasure but then, unbelievably, outrageously, refusing to 'reciprocate.'"[10]

Maggie Nelson has argued that the desire to be a bottom—to be "self-forgetful, incautious, overwhelmed" during sex—needs to be honored not only among straight people but also among queer people and people of all genders.[11] So too, she explains, does the desire to "consume, top, penetrate, or fetishize" need to be untethered from its associations with cis men. But she also acknowledges the tricky business of figuring out "how to honor and allow for [these] drive[s] in a world full of crappy gendered dynamics."[12] Pushing Nelson's analysis further, we can recognize that the cultural meanings associated with sexual one-sidedness are deeply gendered and cannot be separated from their structural context: no one calls a straight man who lays back for a blowjob without reciprocation a "pillow princess," though we should. Patriarchy codes men's sexual selfishness as agency or natural aggression, and women's as passivity and laziness. In a gender-binary erotic system, giving pleasure is feminine or women's work, whereas demanding, and consuming, pleasure is an entitlement of male biology.

But lesbians and other queers—refuseniks of the patriarchal symbolic order—have long asserted our right to recode and re-gender nonreciprocal sex. There is perhaps no better example of the distinctly different meaning of lesbian sexual one-sidedness than femme-butch sexual norms of the mid-twentieth century. Although critics of femme-butch often describe it as a mimicry of heterosexual gender roles, it is more accurate to say that its subculture turned hetero norms upside down, especially when it came to sex. Butches, masculine in their dress and mannerisms, typically derived pleasure from acts of sexual service or from giving pleasure to eager and demanding femmes. In *The Persistent Desire: A Femme-Butch Reader*, Elizabeth Kennedy and Madeline Davis describe this arrangement:

> Features of lesbian erotic culture distinguished it sharply from the heterosexual world. First, the butch-fem erotic system did not consistently follow the gender divisions of the dominant society. The active, or "masculine," partner was associated with the giving of sexual pleasure, a service usually assumed [in the heterosexual world] to be "feminine." In contrast, the fem . . . demanded and received sexual pleasure. . . . Second, the butch's pleasure was always connected to the act of giving; her ability to pleasure her fem was the key to her own satisfaction. This was not true of men.[13]

In fact, in the working-class, femme-butch erotic culture of the 1940s and 1950s, the more masculine the butch, the less inclined she was to receive sexual pleasure; the term "stone butch," for instance, referred to very masculine women who enjoyed pleasuring femmes but who refused to be touched sexually themselves. There was, and is, no corollary for this kind of masculinity in straight sexual culture, and this tells us a great deal about the differences between female masculinity and heteromasculinity, lesbian sex and straight sex. In lesbian sexual culture—a subculture always already infused with antipatriarchal rebellion—the ability to serve women, to make women come, is a powerful badge of honor, one that sometimes supersedes the interests of one's own body.

Can, or should, sex be offered as a gift, without the expectation that the gift will be repaid? Most of us would likely agree that it is more rewarding to offer a gift to someone who hasn't already hounded us into giving it, or when the gift is a generous offering rather than an act of duty. Lesbian friends and acquaintances have shared stories with me about times when they offered sex as a favor or a gift to a woman, despite some degree of disinterest or without enthusiasm, because giving sexual pleasure to another woman—especially in a culture that denies women pleasure, discourages women's desire, and misrecognizes and hates women's bodies—felt like a queer and feminist act of care or solidarity, not an act of obligation or subservience.[14] When sex is an act of erotic solidarity, when it is not overdetermined by heteropatriarchy and men's entitlement, the complexities of sexual service and the collective and political stakes of providing pleasure to women come into clearer view.

Efforts to create a uniform standard for what counts as ethical, feminist sex are bound to be plagued by the fact that people have sex under varying levels of patriarchal constraint, and hence require divergent feminist principles as their guides. The careful regulation of power differentials through enthusiastic consent and sexual egalitarianism is flawed, but these approaches may offer the best path forward for straight women, given their location within heterosexuality's rigged system.[15] They need not also be queer women's guiding star, however, because we are operating in a context in which power and one-sidedness have different gendered meanings.

Much is possible when patriarchy is not the context in which women are being fucked.

Notes

1. Of course, lesbians live under patriarchy, too, but our sexual encounters are not beholden to it. In lesbian sex, activities that produce women's orgasms are not ancillary or deemed "foreplay." Lesbian sex does not end when a man has come. Male biology— the so-called unstoppable urges, the blue balls—is not the ground on which lesbians stake our claim to sexual fulfillment. So, even though straight people need a new set of feminist sex rules that can undermine rape culture and men's sexual entitlement, we need not imagine that these rules will be seamlessly applicable to queer sex.

2. Tarana Burke, *Unbound: My Story of Liberation and the Birth of the MeToo Movement* (New York: Flatiron Books, 2021); Brittney Cooper, *Eloquent Rage: A Black Feminist Discovers Her Superpower* (New York: St Martin's Press, 2018); Gloria González-López, *Family Secrets: Stories of Incest and Sexual Violence in Mexico* (New York: NYU Press, 2015); and Jane Ward, *The Tragedy of Heterosexuality* (New York: NYU Press, 2020).

3. Rebecca Traister, "The Game Is Rigged: Why Consensual Sex Can Still Be Bad," *New York Magazine*, October 20, 2015, http://nymag.com/thecut/2015/10/why-consensual-sex-can-still -be-bad.html.

4. Reina Gattuso, "What I Would Have Said to You Last Night Had You Not Cum and then Fallen Asleep," *Feministing*, January 19, 2016, http://feministing.com/2016/01/19/what-i -would-have-said-to-you-last-night-had-you-not-cum-and-then -fallen-asleep/.

5. Nicola Gavey, *Just Sex? The Cultural Scaffolding of Rape* (London: Routledge, 2005).

6. Maggie Nelson, *On Freedom: Four Songs of Care and Constraint* (New York: Graywolf Press, 2021), 95.

7. Laura Harris, "Confessions of the Pillow Queen: Sexual Receptivity & Queer Femininities," in *Tribades, Tommies, and Transgressives: Histories of Sexualities: Vol. I*, ed. Mary McAuliffe and Sonja Tiernan (Dublin: Cambridge Scholars Press, 2008), 272.

8. Harris, "Confessions of the Pillow Queen," 272.

9. Harris, "Confessions of the Pillow Queen," 278.

10. Harris, "Confessions of the Pillow Queen," 271.

11. Nelson, *On Freedom*, 95.

12. Nelson, *On Freedom*, 95–96.

13. Joan Nestle, *The Persistent Desire: A Femme–Butch Reader* (New York: Alyson Books, 1992).

14. I am thinking here about adriene maree brown's treatise on "pleasure activism," which illuminates the ways that pleasure is denied people with structural power and calls for social justice movements to redistribute opportunities for pleasure.

15. Juana Maria Rodriguez, *Sexual Futures, Queer Gestures, and Other Latina Longings* (New York: NYU Press, 2014); Joseph Fischel, *Screw Consent: A Better Politics of Sexual Justice* (Oakland: University of California Press, 2019).

5

Momentos de consentimiento

Consent in Lesbian Relationships
in Mexico City

GLORIA GONZÁLEZ-LÓPEZ AND
ANAHI RUSSO GARRIDO

GLORIA: Buenos días, good morning. Thank you for accepting
my invitation to have this conversation on consent in
lesbian relationships in Mexico City. I read your book
*Tortilleras Negotiating Intimacy: Love, Friendship, and Sex
in Queer Mexico City*. I was familiar with your dissertation
project, but I had the opportunity to read the book—
thank you for your work. So, the conversation I would like
to have with you today is also based on what I learned
from you after reading the book. Also, the conversation
I would like to have is about cisgender women; my understanding is that the women that you interviewed were
predominantly cisgender . . . [and two transgender women
who participated in lesbian circles]. So, I just wanted
to ask you to remind me again of the timeline of your
research. So, then I can think of what's also happening
historically in the country.

ANAHI: Yeah. So, for the master's thesis, I conducted research mostly in the year 2000–2001. For the PhD, I did most of the interviews in 2009–2010. And then for the book, I continued until 2016, although most of the interviews were in 2009–2010, but conversations continued until 2016. . . . I defended my dissertation in 2012.

GLORIA: 2012, okay. I forgot. Yeah. I'm just thinking about your own transformation, your own evolution, all these twenty years with regard to consent. The biggest surprise as a researcher, what is it?

ANAHI: I think that consent in Mexico is connected to models of heterosexuality that imagine men as desiring and women as recipients of this desire. One of the people I interviewed who is named Selene, a student in history, said, "Women have always been assigned a passive role." She was talking about how her sexual education was different than the one of her brother. She said as a woman you are taught that "you have to wait to be seduced; someone arrives, they flirt, and even if you like it, you deny it three times before responding." And I found that interesting that she was saying you deny it three times before responding even if you're interested. You have to really stick to that script of not being so interested in sexuality, being passive. And so, the idea of consent really connects, right, with this model where the woman has to deny three times before she says, "Okay, yes, I'm interested." This sexual script would suggest that women have to protect themselves and men have to insist. I think in the lesbian context, this script is not there in the same way. The script in terms of who will make the first move, who will be interested or disinterested is not there. Now does that mean that all these scripts drop between lesbians? Obviously not. What also comes to mind is that we could think of consenting as always an active act, an agreement between people to engage in sexual acts because they want to engage in it. This questions this gendered script in some ways. But, in terms of who will be approaching the other, who will be saying yes, who will be saying no, do you have to say yes right away? The script is not as clear between women, because the dominant script is heteronormative.

GLORIA: So, this is really interesting because there's a couple of contexts here. There's the context of the more stable monogamous relationship, right? There's thinking of also women who share a space, who live together. And then there's the women who are not in a relationship necessarily, but who are dating and then how to negotiate the so-called consent. And people use it; it's actually really interesting, to say, "*Yo no di mi consentimiento*": you know, "I didn't give my consent." But then, how is it negotiated? And actually, and this is always the critique, can people negotiate that? I mean now that people talk about the enthusiastic consent like "Yessss!" In real life, what does that "saying yes" . . . look like? Like you were saying something like, "Who's gonna make the first move?" And then how people respond to that first move. And, so I just wanted to see if we could explore that more.

ANAHI: I have to say that the script that I was describing is the traditional script. Like, we know that in everyday life it's more complex in heterosexual or same-sex or various sex relationships, in terms of who makes the first move. There is the dominant script that everyone recognizes and then there's how it really happens. And among these scripts there is also, as you were saying, the script of what a relationship should look like between two people —*una relación de pareja.* One of my interlocutors named Claudia talks about how a couple she is friends with gave themselves *pequeños permisos,* small permissions. And she says for example, that that couple would allow themselves to kiss other girls at bars. And so, the term *permisos*. I'm wondering how that informs consent or defers from consent, right? To give permission to someone is to consent to it. But, also in permission there is a particular authority. So, in this example, this person is consenting for their partner to kiss other women at a bar. But it is not framed under the word "consent," which I think is more of a legal term. This is a moment where they're talking about consent through the word *permisos*, that *permiso a tu pareja* [is] permission to your partner to do something that is not part of the mainstream social contract in a relationship.

GLORIA: One of the concepts that I use with my students is the "Aha!" the aha moments. The aha moments that you have as a researcher on how women then negotiate. And it's actually so interesting, and we know this as researchers and based on my own personal experiences, this idea of consent, to what extent is based on cognition? So, if you could share your aha moments, your research surprises, important lessons on, you know, what you've learned from these women who shared their stories with you . . . [What were moments where people said "yes" or "no"?]

ANAHI: The "yes I wanted to do it." I'm thinking of an interview with a woman who was married to her high school sweetheart for about ten to fifteen years. And she talks about how she began having an affair with a woman while she was married. She was married and it was, at that time, the 1990s when you couldn't go online to see which lesbian organizations were meeting or forming a community on social media. And she was watching TV with her husband, and one evening a lesbian activist on TV talked about her experiences as a lesbian and then said, "If you need help, please reach out to this phone number." And she was with her husband in bed, and she said she memorized the phone number. It would be too obvious if she wrote it down. And so, she calls the next day; she starts going to this space. She meets a woman. And then, when she talks about "Yes, I want to do it," she describes the first time she had sex with a woman. In the book, she says "Ay, imagine, waiting so many years to be with a woman. It was the best. To be able to feel her breasts, her intimate parts, to kiss her, which was what turned me on the most. It was a completely different emotion." And so that was a moment of "yes," like something that was, by social norms, forbidden, that she had not permitted herself. Despite all social scripts that were against what she felt, right?

And then, a moment of "no" that I can think of that comes up in the book is when one of the interlocutors nicknamed Monkey talks about casual sex. And she does not talk about it as not wanting to do it, but in retrospect she does. She was ending a seven-year relationship and was trying to find herself and was having a hard time. And she began going out every night to a club, and she talks about how during that period of her life, she would have casual sex with different people. And when I asked her, if she liked casual sex, she said, "It disgusts me; how could I do that? You don't know with who you're going to sleep with. You don't know if they may be dangerous," etc. So that's interesting because there's consent in the moment, but also in retrospect, she felt disgust. I think that she points to these moments where it seemed evident, but in retrospect, she doesn't feel good about it and wishes she didn't engage in those sexual interactions. There could be a little bit of the discourse of the good/bad woman engaging in casual sex here. But overall, she's very categorical, expressing that she felt disgust, which is a pretty strong word. It wasn't "Oh I didn't feel good about it" or "I'm not sure if I should have done it"; it was "It disgusts me."

GLORIA: Yeah, so the consent and then regret.

ANAHI: Right. There are moments of "no" also I think, when we think about people who have sex with people of the gender that they don't want to have sex with. So, for example, when some of the women were younger and if they were not interested in men, and they did it because that's what they were supposed to be doing. So it goes into various degrees, right? So, there's the consent when they decide to engage in it, but deep down inside, were they really enthusiastic about it, right? So that's, again, not about categorically saying no, but complying with the social norms that expect you to be sexual and to be sexual with people of a certain gender in a gender-binary world.

GLORIA: Yes, that reminds me of what I learned from my first book project: I learned a lot about the mythology of heterosexuality. . . . But as I'm listening to you, what do you think of this idea of moments of consent? Like if we could break it down, there's some refined moments. There's a moment. And then in those moments, I'm also thinking about, and please share with me, the role of seduction; you know, if you're being seduced . . . now I'm thinking. Probably we can talk about these moments of consent, especially for people who are dating. Like when people go out to *La Zona Rosa*, and I'm just being stereotypical here, but you can go to other places, other lesbian spaces in Mexico City. And there's the dim light and then there's some music, and then you're dating and then the other person is also dating. All of these moments of seduction. Based on your own research, what did you learn?

ANAHI: Yeah. I think that you're right that there is a *moment-by-moment* interaction in which people will look for cues, right? Is the other person interested? And unless you're at a certain type of college in the United States, there's not an established protocol of "Do you want to have sex?" and then the other person has to verbalize it. It is not as rehearsed as that, and people will be looking for forms of confirmation, right? Maybe the bodies lean toward each other. Maybe one person puts their hand on the shoulder of the other and sees if the person stays there or if they move back. Consent, thinking about it moment by moment, also reflects a certain number of steps that will take place before people kiss, for example. And there are spaces where the temporality of consent is accelerated. At a bar where there's a dance floor, people may come closer to each other faster, and there are ways in which it is permitted to come closer to each other. Dancing particular songs of, I don't know, salsa, cumbia, where you're allowed to touch each other. But even then, there are limits to how you can touch each other, where you can put your hands or not. So, I think that there's different spaces where there are different temporalities of consent. We could think about a dance floor versus a workspace, for example. The temporality of it is probably very, very slow and delicate because of the way things are codified, even from a legal standpoint. People who meet each other at lesbian groups might gaze at another woman to see if there is interest. They might invite the other to some activity, etc., before any intimate possibility. Things happening moment to moment to moment. I'm thinking that there are different temporalities of that *moment-to-moment* consent that is embedded in some social scripts that exist in these spaces.

GLORIA: And so then, based on your own research, to what extent is alcohol consumption part of those experiences? You were talking about temporality or . . . this *micro-chronology*.

It's just like, if we had it like in slow motion, right? [laughs] And then you go like, "Okay so now poof!" That's when they kind of accepted to say yes, and then, and then they decide. And then they take care of the logistics. The logistics come later. You know, we go to your place, go to my place, go to the car, whatever. So that's like the logistics of, you know. But then this chronology, it's very delicate. It's actually very delicate. It's very refined. It's actually really, incredibly refined. Based on your research, what did you learn about alcohol and alcohol consumption in these lesbian communities, in these cultures?

ANAHI: I'm sure that it happens. It seems like a plausible story, but I'm trying to think of a concrete moment where someone in the book or in an article says, "I drank so much and I, I got into that, I had sex with this person." I don't have a concrete story that I can think of here.

GLORIA: And then uh, so then I'm thinking, you know, legally have you ever heard cases of women—in all these years that you've been conducting research on lesbian relationships with lesbian activists—who have followed a legal process . . . [when] accusing another woman of sexual violence? Have you heard that?

ANAHI: I have not heard of a case or anything that became prominent in the media or the community, but it can occur.

GLORIA: Mmhmm.

ANAHI: I was reading an article by a journalist named Abril Torres. She had conversations with five people who identify as lesbians who were in violent relationships.[1] And she talks about how she didn't find so many cases of how we imagine sexual violence as rape or like this type of expression, but she found a lot of moments of control and obligation in the lives of the women she interviewed. One of her interlocutors talks about how she felt that she couldn't decide when she wanted to be sexual; it was only the other partner who would decide. And so that's a moment of control that we can connect to this idea of violence. And there was another person who also talked about the other partner making the decisions about what they would do. So, she doesn't say that she did not at that moment consent to it, but that in retrospect, she realized she was in a violent relationship and she did not have a say in their sexual life. So that relates also to this idea of sexual violence and consent and obligation.

GLORIA: Yeah. So, . . . what you're sharing with me then is teaching me a lesson on how women in an abusive lesbian relationship may make sense of their experiences of sexual violence.

ANAHI: In my research, I have some examples of economic violence. Of people who were in the model of one person works and the other doesn't. And then the person who doesn't work wanted to end the relationship, but the other person would always bring her more expensive gifts to keep her there like, "Oh, here's a new electronic piano, and here is this new video game console, and here is this . . ." And so I do have some examples of violence in lesbian relationships in my research, but this person that I'm thinking of does not necessarily describe sexual violence in her relationship.

GLORIA: I think it's more like, people . . . feel more comfortable saying, "Yeah, it was emotional violence." Even if it involved sexualized violence or sexual violence or sexual coercion. But it's the emotional violence, it fits, it feels kind of comfortable. It's just like, "Yeah, she was emotionally violent."

ANAHI: Yeah, I would think so. And it's not an accident that I'm talking about sexual violence because I feel really that's part of the vocabulary that is used to talk about ideas of consent. It comes from feminist organizations and lesbian organizations that have workshops on those topics. And also . . . that's media-ized language to talk about gender-based violence. People, at least the ones I interviewed, went to some of the support meetings and groups that had some of that language.

GLORIA: Yeah, I remember I attended a support group for women in lesbian relationships in summer 2006, and . . . I think all of them were attending because they had some history of being in an abusive lesbian relationship. And it was, it was really interesting to listen to—especially as I'm listening to you and I'm thinking about that presentation: there's all the professionalization, all of the language that people use to make sense of all of this. So, then there are professional cultures that have established a language to talk about, and consent is part of that. Consent is one of the concepts, right? And then lesbian activists who are highly . . . involved in human rights movements or feminist movements or feminist groups, then they have all this language and professional language. And then they share that language with all of these lesbian groups, and then there's the lesbian woman who's learning. And then she knows that something doesn't feel right in this relationship. And then she uses that language to make sense of it. You know, so it's actually really, really interesting. It would be really interesting to see how, as you continue doing research on this . . . to see how that is going to evolve, you know, the language, and then the ways in which these professionals talk about all these expressions of pain and inequality, etc.

So, with these reflections on being in the moment, we can use this terminology. . . . Oh, by the way, I am out as a Buddhist; are you out as a Buddhist?

ANAHI: Yes, I am out as a Buddhist . . . I am actually writing a paper about race, Buddhism, and social justice endeavors.

GLORIA: So, thank you for sharing. As you know, the idea is for this essay to be of help to future readers, and I think this idea of what happens to us when we are paying attention to the moment is important when it comes to consent.

ANAHI: It's interesting that you are bringing up all that, the moment by moment; I have been thinking about that regarding social justice issues. I am teaching a Meditation and Social Justice Activism course now. I have been thinking about how you may think you have some ideas about a particular issue in a very cerebral, cognitive way. But if you begin really exploring it—and I am thinking about the literature on race and Buddhism that talks about what goes on in your mind moment by moment, with your body, your bodily sensations, moment by moment—you might see that you are maybe uncomfortable with certain parts of an issue you thought you were supportive of, or that you have contradictory thoughts about it. I think that there are circumstances in which consent operates similarly. Hopefully, it is very clear if you want to engage in sex. But really looking at it, moment by moment, and [your] bodily reactions and sensations, it can become more complex, if people feel comfortable with particular interactions or sexual gestures. And I think it becomes more complex when you slow down and really see what goes on in your mind and body, moment by moment, breath by breath.

GLORIA: This is great—thank you. It is so fascinating that both of us have a connection with Buddhism. So this idea of paying attention to what is happening to you at the moment and to explore to what extent you are aware—or not—of what is happening to you in your mind. And that is why alcohol is a concern. So, it is interesting how we ended up with this idea of moment to moment without talking openly about Buddhism.

And thank you for sharing the Abril Torres piece on violence in lesbian relationships. She was so courageous to publish this article. With regard to sexual violence in lesbian relationships I have been exposed to two discourses, narratives, or perspectives. One of them is not to talk about it: "We get along OK; we are struggling for whatever cause; that is not a priority at the moment so we should not talk about it." It is not politically correct, so we don't talk about it. And the second one is where Abril Torres seems to be coming from: it is this idea that the concerns about sexual violence against women are exclusionary, it is about ciswomen in heterosexual relationships. When I was in Mexico City doing my fieldwork in 2006, the latter [perspective] was already becoming the dominant narrative, but I do not know how early these conversations started to take place. I wonder about how these ideas have evolved in lesbian circles.

ANAHI: Yeah, I remember group meetings with Musas de Metal, a queer organization, and they had a workshop on violence in couples. They went through definitions of violence, different types of violence, so people could reflect and talk about it. So, it is a conversation that has been there for some years. I have been looking for statistics on violence in relationships, but I could not find a recent one that would take into account sexual identity in Mexico,[2] but I found a short survey that Musas de Metal did during COVID.

GLORIA: So, during COVID relationship violence has gone up for heterosexual couples, and it has gone up for lesbian couples as well.

ANAHI: Yes, according to the study by Musas de Metal.

GLORIA: So, the pandemic has affected everyone. So, there is no vaccine in the queer world to be protected from relationship violence.

ANAHI: Correct, but the study speaks of violence at home. Not only for couples.

GLORIA: So, going back to consent, I am thinking about the idea of women feeling comfortable with their bodies, if they would have some sort of "selective consent," as in, "Yes, but like this." I remember some men in my research complaining about women not feeling comfortable with their bodies or women wearing all these layers of pajamas, especially if it is cold. So, I just wanted to know if you could share more about what people shared with you with regard to these issues.

ANAHI: Yes, I remember one of the women commenting on her body changing, especially with age, and health issues, in her forties. After having health issues, she got heavier . . . : "So I was *gordita pero me veía bien*—I was chubby, but I looked OK." But with ten pounds more she felt uncomfortable with her body and how that impacted her desire to engage in sex. So, her relationship to her body changed, and she was less interested in sex, although her partner was still interested in it.

GLORIA: Thank you for sharing the story. Or, negotiating certain things . . . like, I was thinking about people negotiating based on comfort. For example, "I will have sex with you but only with the lights off." Or identifying the bedroom as the only place to have sex. Those are only examples. So, this is about negotiating sexual engagements based on comfort, and again, it is about consent. Anything on that?

ANAHI: Actually, I am thinking about stories that are about being out in public and showing public affection. For a couple, it was "Yes in the bedroom but don't come near me in public." So, there is a form of consent, in private but not in public. Women that I interviewed had to face that reality, that some of the women they were [with were] not out in public. That is a negotiation that is not always well seen in the community. So, if the person is not willing, she is read as "¡Oh! es de closet—Oh! she is in the closet." So, there is pressure to be out, and that is a moment that I am thinking where things are negotiated not in the bedroom but in public spaces.

GLORIA: So, these are intimate negotiations that are lived in public, or that happen in a public space, or may even involve the community—like holding hands in public, kissing, I think of those two. As you know, women relate to their bodies in different ways across cultures. So, it is interesting what you share because in Mexico, in general, women feel comfortable with physical closeness, kissing on the cheek, hugging in public, etc. I have also noticed that women may walk together; you know, like when I walk with my mom, I bend my arm, and she puts her hand in the crook of my elbow and has some support while we walk side by side. And I have seen mature women in lesbian relationships who do the same in public, so it is a way to be close but also discrete about it. . . . I was going to ask you about women who were in heterosexual relationships in the past and now they are in a relationship with a woman: Did that shape their sexual experiences with women? How does that shape consent?

ANAHI: An interlocutor told me that her lover who had been married to a man was frozen and did not know what to do during sex, and she had a discussion with her and she said, "Well, there is no manual or special book for that; you do what you feel." And that way her girlfriend had more room to be spontaneous, to explore sex. So, this idea that there was no script or a book that would tell her exactly what to do with a woman. But I don't know in terms of consent how that would work. When did we consent to that social script we were given? Women are socialized to not consent until marriage, in the more traditional plot. In a lesbian context, I am thinking of a quote by an interlocutor, Selene: "If women go to a bar, and all [the] women are waiting around to be seduced, and everyone is waiting because they have been socialized to wait, then nothing happens." And she is a little bit making fun of that situation, not meaning that it is exactly like that. I am thinking of scholar Ana Amuchástegui's idea of the "self-acknowledgment of desire" and then taking the steps to do it. It is like boys are socialized to "Yeah! Go talk to her!" but you as a woman are not encouraged to do that.

GLORIA: So, in this conversation the paradigm that has come up is this idea of paying attention to the moment . . . moments of desire, moments of consent, and taking literally one moment at a time. But then the thing is that we are not aware of all this actually happening. And [when we] become aware of it, then that is this "self-acknowledgement of desire." But then the question is, because we live in a patriarchal society, to what extent do we even have the right to acknowledge desire? And this question is for lesbian, bisexual, queer women, for all ciswomen, I think. So, to what extent does patriarchy not allow us to claim that right to acknowledge desire, and then pursue it, or to say no, not now, not at this moment?

ANAHI: Actually, the concept is "self-authorization of desire," my mistake . . .

GLORIA: OK, no problem . . . but that makes it even more interesting, because before the authorization has to happen, we need to have some sort of acknowledgment anyway, correct? It is actually interesting that some Mexican women—scholars included—may use these concepts to make sense of sexuality and relationship-related processes: *permisos, acuerdos, autorización*—permission, agreements, authorization. It is like our sexual lives (and how we make sense of them) are framed within these ideas of an official authority and obedience, approval, sanctions, rules of conduct, licenses, norms, etc. And then consent is framed within these frameworks. Anyway . . . the acknowledgment requires awareness, and the authorization comes next, and it is about having the right to move on.

ANAHI: Yeah. you are right. And the acknowledgment goes with this idea of being moment to moment, and being aware of my desires, but you are not even socialized to acknowledge them.

GLORIA: Yesss. So, these ideas of the *acuerdo* also with regard to sexual encounters . . .

ANAHI: There is a quote in the book: an interlocutor, Vanesa says she has dated married women, and she says, "OK, you can see me on weekends because you are with your family during the week and that is OK." So that is an agreement that she is making with that person.

GLORIA: Interesting. One of the important themes with regard to consent that also comes to mind has to do with body ability, and here I am thinking about lesbian women who use wheelchairs, lesbian women who may have disabilities.

ANAHI: I don't think that it is an explicit conversation, but it comes up in a segment I mentioned about having health problems and not being able to engage in sex as in the past. And so that's about body ability, and here we are talking about how imaginaries of sex are attached to sex with able bodies in a particular period of life that would function in ways that conceptualize it as this idea of intercourse. I did not find it to be a central conversation in the community, but I am certain it is there. I am also thinking that the spaces where the meetings took place were not spaces where people, let's say with mobility issues, would be able to come to. I know that disabilities are not only about mobility issues but I am just thinking about that now.

GLORIA: So, I also wanted to ask you, based on your research, what does sexual coercion look like in *el ambiente*, in queer circles in Mexico City? I know that these are not easy conversations. . . . You and I read the piece by Abril Torres, but I just wanted to know if you could reflect more on it.

ANAHI: I am not sure if I have something to add to that, but in Torres's article, one of the interviewees said she did not think before that it [sexual coercion] could happen between women. So, I think on one level there is that, and at another level there are organizations that are talking about violence in lesbian relationships and that could include sexual coercion. At the first level it could be not having the traditional language of those workshops to articulate it. So, it does not always look like what you might learn in a training about sexual coercion.

GLORIA: But you were explaining that people are talking about it.

ANAHI: Yes, in organizations and support groups. I remember a workshop at Musas de Metal and also in the group Mayores de 30—Older than 30—and probably other organizations. But these two for sure.

GLORIA: So, then there is the question about the #MeToo . . . queering the #MeToo, and the question is if you think that some aspects of these lesbian cultures create particular dynamics for consent. And this is interesting because of the informants in the article by Abril Torres talk about the #MeToo. So, I wonder if you could share a queer

#MeToo story. And we know that the #MeToo kicked off in October 2017. So, anything relevant to the #MeToo within lesbian circles?

ANAHI: No, not directly around the #MeToo, or the *#MeTooEscritoresMexicanos.* It has been highly heterosexualized. But organizations are talking about how sexual violence is directed toward lesbians and how that is silenced. When you do a search with "sexual violence and lesbians in Mexico" you find a lot about "corrective rapes"[3] or the ways in which lesbians are sexually harassed for being lesbians. . . . One of my interlocutors, a software engineer, was harassed at work. Her boss was a woman and was interested in her, but she was not interested in her. It became public, and people at work started harassing her and saying, "Oh, you are the boss's favorite; that's why you got that contract." She became a target when it became public information at work; it created a hostile environment. She told me the story in 2011, and the events happened around 2009 or 2008.

GLORIA: So, that case was years before the #MeToo. But these are important reflections about how the #MeToo has become heterosexualized in Mexico, at least, based on what you and I have learned about it. So . . . for the purposes of this essay, we need to wrap it up. Are we missing anything with regard to consent and lesbian relationships?

ANAHI: *Hay mucha tela que cortar*—there is much to discuss on this topic. Some of the concepts that have been the most interesting in the conversation . . . some ideas that I think are central, that can mobilize the conversation, include body ability, accessibility but body availability too. The idea of the *permisos* . . . so there have been some conceptual moments useful to work around.

GLORIA: So, we have body ability and *body availability*, as in "I am not available," or "I am not available at this moment." Sorry, I hope I did not interrupt your train of thought..

ANAHI: Oh, no, no. Or like the "moment to moment" idea.

GLORIA: So, we have body ability, body availability, moments of consent, and moments of desire. So, we are always navigating moments of consent and moments of desire. Anything challenging or difficult to discuss?

ANAHI: So, I think like you were saying that when doing research with people, people are not always open to these discussions. How do people talk about consent in their everyday life and not only in legal terms? Like I said, #MeToo had an impact in Mexico but there were other hashtags that circulated more, like *#NiUnaMás*. So, there is a work of translation: it is not that people don't talk about consent, or that people don't talk about sexual violence, or that #MeToo was not important, but that there are ways of talking about it in everyday life that are not in that particular social science language or in a more U.S.-based language. So that has been the most challenging . . . to identify, this is similar to this concept.

GLORIA: So, it is the conceptual translation, and all the stuff that gets lost in translation. Those of us who do research on the Mexican side and then publish in English, and then teach in English . . . work not only on the conceptual translation but the cultural translation, as in "this is what it means." And there is the stuff that gets lost in translation, and that is beautiful; I like that because that means that it cannot be translated. And people may say "I don't get it" and I say, "Great! Precisely what you don't get is what makes it so unique."

ANAHI: Yeah. Also, what you mentioned earlier, consent as an idea is around cognitive processes and this idea that words won't capture necessarily fully what goes on in the mind of someone, or the experiences that they are having in their body, or the sensations in the process of consenting. Consent is the surface of the iceberg that summarizes if someone is eager to engage in or not. Sometimes it can be very clear; the sensations can be very clear and so on. But there can be gray zones that can be contradictory thoughts, contradictory emotions. And at the same time, we want the clarity, right? We don't want anybody to suffer in the process. So there needs to be that clarity, but at the same time we know that is not always that simple.

GLORIA: Thank you. I hope we are bringing some clarity to be of help to others.

ANAHI: Me too.

En el tinero ~ Yet to be written

We had this dialogue based on our knowledge about specific lesbian cultures in Mexico City; it may not reflect how women in lesbian relationships in other urban Mexican areas and different regions experience their sex lives and consent. We are both aware of the complex ways in which different social forces and processes may further shape what we discussed in our conversation. For instance, consent in lesbian relationships might also be shaped by the following: gender inequality and regional cultures and economies (i.e., *regional patriarchies*); race, ethnic relations, pigmentocracy, and colorism, especially well-established ideologies and practices historically affecting Indigenous and Afro-Mexican people; cultural and ethnic diversity concerns; class relations, privilege, and socioeconomic marginality; dominant Catholic and other nondominant religious affiliations and spiritual practices; different types of disabilities, including but not limited to body ability and limited accessibility in private and public spaces; beauty standards, pop culture, and inequality; polyamory; nightlife cultures including the *cuartos violetas* where some women engage in sexual exchanges; sexual violence against women, legal norms, and heteronormativity; lesbian participation in the feminist movement; and, corrective rape, lesbophobia, *lesboterrorismo*, hate crimes, and *feminicidio* or killings of women rooted in gender inequality (women, who by the way, are frequently assumed to be heterosexual). We explored these topics in our extended conversation but do not include them in this chapter because of space limitations. All these topics deserve in-depth analysis in future examinations on consent. Regardless, we hope the reflections offered here will be of benefit to future readers in their ongoing conversations on consent in *all* relationship arrangements.

With gratitude,
Anahi & Gloria

Notes

This chapter includes only specific themes related to consent, and it is based on two audio-recorded conversations (each lasting two hours) between the authors, which examined a more extended and wider range of topics about lesbian relationships in Mexico City. The conversations took place in July 2021 via Zoom. This verbatim text is an abbreviated version of the original; both authors revised it and incorporated edits and corrections for style. The authors would like to express their gratitude to Jamie O'Quinn for her professional services and support in the process.

1. Abril Torres. "Somos los cuerpos que amamos: violencia de pareja en relaciones lésbicas" (We are the bodies we love: Intimate partner violence in lesbian relationships), May 25, 2021, https://cultura.nexos.com.mx/somos-los-cuerpos-que-amamos -violencia-de-pareja-en-relaciones-lesbicas/.

2. For a report on violence against lesbians in Mexico, see Cervantes Medina, Julio César and Cristina Arévalo Contreras

(coordinators), *Violencia contra lesbianas* (Violence against lesbians). Comisión Nacional de los Derechos Humanos, México, 2020, https://www.cndh.org.mx/sites/default/files /documentos/2021-06/L_Violencia_contra_lesbianas.pdf.

3. "Corrective rape" is a term widely used in South African legal scholarship. It refers to an instance when rape is used to "correct" a person's sexual identity. See, for example, René Koraan and Allison Geduld, "'Corrective Rape' of Lesbians in the Era of Transformative Constitutionalism in South Africa," *Potchefstroom Electronic Law Journal* (PELJ) 18, no. 5 (2015), http://dx.doi.org/10.4314/pelj.v18i5.23.

6

Black Femmedom as Violence and Resistance

MISTRESS VELVET

For many submissive white men, the experience of being owned by Mistress Velvet, a Dominatrix, is a high priority. With fetishes and specialties ranging from corporal punishment to sissification, bondage, and foot fetish, sessions with Velvet work both for novices in the BDSM (bondage and discipline, dominance and submission, sadism and masochism) community and for those with years of experience. She describes Herself as sensual, seductive, and firm, priding Herself on offering safer spaces for individuals to explore their submissive side. Mistress Velvet's clients—Her slaves, pets, subs, house bitches, and fuck bois—are almost exclusively cis-heterosexual (or abashedly hetero-flexible) middle-aged white men who have corporate jobs and identify as alpha males in their "normal" lives. They reach out because of a long-lasting, unsatiated internal sense of submissiveness that they want to explore or grow within.

Many of Her slaves have wives who are either oblivious to this aspect of their husband's sexual desires or are repulsed by the thought of it. Most of Her pets feel a deep sense of shame about their beta tendencies, for despite their desires they still subscribe heavily to normative standards of masculinity. Many of those who seek out Mistress Velvet also have an untamed fascination with and fixation on being owned by a woman who is Black and, in many cases, African. That is, they are not satisfied with merely transgressing their binary gender norms but are also enticed by the crossing of racial borders. Although Mistress Velvet is one of the few Dommes of Color—much less Black Dommes—in Her city, Her specialty of Black femme supremacy and white male inferiority is in demand.

Over the past few years, I have crafted and cultivated my persona as Mistress Velvet, based on a deep exploration of my personal kinks and boundaries and an examination of the internalized notions that I have reluctantly carried in my flesh. Although I have engaged in other types of sex work, I now exclusively work as a femdom (female domination) provider for submissive white men. My domination may take many forms, but its foundations lie in a race play that focuses on the ownership and enslavement of white men. This literal playing with and disrupting standard racial comforts and scripts work in conjunction with my femdom to upset systems of straight, cisgender, white male hegemony; it lurks on the fringes of erotic performativity—a perversion rife with history and trauma. Yet, the intersections of being a professional dominatrix who is also a revolutionary feminist means that I often vacillate between feeding into the fetishes, tropes, and exotifications that are specific to my clientele and critiquing the very kind of BDSM that I engage with.

Although the practice of BDSM exists on the margins of idealized, puritan heterosexuality, it has been a site of growth, contradiction, and resistance for understanding my race, gender, and sexuality. A consistent assumption that others make is that the expression of a dominant Black sexuality and the owning of white male slaves are inherently empowering. I speculate that some others would disagree, arguing that Mistress Velvet's power over submissive white men does not necessarily challenge or radically change stereotypes and tropes of Black femininity, nor does the inversion of power result in the dismantling of oppressive norms. In some ways, I agree. To regard Mistress Velvet as powerful necessitates an othering that is fixated not only on Her perceived difference(s) from other Black women but also on Black women's relationship to the arguably immutable category of (white) womanhood. The choice made by clients to be submissive to a Black woman is a product of the Eurocentric fetishization of women of Color. My value as a Domme comes from a fluid yet dualistic construction of me as different (read: institutionally educated, attractive, accessible) from other Black women, yet also different (read: racially and sexually exotic) from white women. When submissives make statements about choosing me because I am smart or not ghetto, they are conceptualizing me as an anomaly to Black femmehood. When they insist on Black female superiority over white women, they are relegating us to a mysteriousness rooted in colonialism. This is where the fallacy of Black femdom empowerment lies. Being a Dominatrix is not inherently liberatory even if it has social currency.

This does not mean that femdom and BDSM do not provide a valuable and critical space in which Black women can center ourselves and define what consent looks like for us. Where many fall short is in a narrow interpretation of liberatory images and the subsequent dismissal of all forms of resistance that do not look like the kind of empowerment they envision. In this case, I am less interested in devaluing work that arguably may or may not institute systemic change and am more invested in elevating the multifaceted ways in which Black women can experience liberation and consensuality, both individually and collectively. I believe that Black femdom—particularly the kind of race play that I engage in, Black femme domination over white male submissives—is a site of inversion that can bring forth pleasure, catharsis, and healing. The establishment of Black women's sexual excess—a trope that we see repeatedly throughout our history—is a foundational technology in this erotic interaction, because its perversion is reclaimed and recuperated for our benefits. Although the power possessed in these instances is not radically redistributed from white supremacy, the co-optation of our abject sexuality for the development of a Black Dommehood within BDSM is one of the few spaces where our sexuality can be used on our terms. I see Black femme sexuality as a peripheral sexuality, and BDSM as a space where peripheral sexualities can exist.

Who is to say what quantity of radicalism Black femme healing represents? Is not the notion of our self-love radical in and of itself? Colonialism disposed of our flesh and clothed us instead with a criminally counterfeit simulacrum of Black femmehood. To undo this work, acknowledge our scars, and love ourselves in spite of it all is supernatural. To then foster a collective and community for other Black femmes who want to find healing in this way is resistance. The epistemological and pedagogical erasure of Black womanhood is an historically embedded process that continues to shape and distort our understandings of what it means to be Black and woman. Certainly, our skin has been degenerated to the point that our (non)gender(s) and (a)sexualities are barely cognizant. The reconstruction of our discursive subjectivity—at the very least on an individual level—is a crucial step in our collective resistance against oppression. This work can only be done by and for Black women and femmes, because Western attempts to make room for our voice further reinforce our silence.

Mistress Velvet ends every session by reminding Her slaves of the burden of their submission. Once a slave has entered into a contract with Mistress, he relinquishes aspects of himself not only to Her but also to every Black woman he encounters. It becomes his duty to reevaluate the ways in which he interacts with us. Mistress Velvet uses a combination of theoretical study and obedience training to educate Her slaves and mandate that they recognize and actively work to unlearn their racist fetishizations and unpack their anti-Black misogyny. At the beginning of each session, the slave recounts his interactions with Black femmes, in whatever capacity they may be, since the last time he shared space with Velvet. He is forced to explain what work he did to subvert Black femme oppression rather than perpetuate it. These ventures have varied from slaves purposefully opening doors only for Black women to pets starting foundations for homeless Black mothers. These are not radical changes, because they are rooted in a chauvinism that is everlasting.

These are the ideological limitations of my work. Their niceties to other Black femmes are rooted in the same misogynoir that keeps them engaging in a race play with a persona I laboriously embody. My niche of BDSM and sex work could not be sustainable without the specific kind of fetishization that I am instructing them to unlearn. The irony lies in the fact that their desires to submit to a Black woman is a consequence of their misogyny. The homework I provide them and the unpacking that I impose on them cannot bring forth an abolition of our oppression. Despite these restrictions, our existence is so fraught with repression that there is pleasure in claiming every minuscule liberatory space and process available to us. It is for this reason that being Mistress

Velvet has been such a source of healing in my life. Having nuance about the work I do allows me to both critique and enjoy its many aspects. Although there is much to analyze, it ultimately serves as a site for me to confront white supremacy and find unique ways to challenge my internalized notions about my race, gender, and sexuality. Alice Walker once said, "Healing begins where the wound was made."[1] For me, Mistress Velvet is both a site of violence and a site of resistance.

Note

1. Alice Walker, *The Way Forward Is with a Broken Heart* (New York: Random House, 2000), 200.

7

Consent through My Lens

A Photo Essay

DON (D. S.) TRUMBULL

As a photographer and active member of the leather + fetish community for the past eight years, I think about consent a lot. I am grateful to be a part of a community that can offer seemingly unlimited resources for thinking through what consent looks like and how to practice it.

Consent regularly comes into play when I photograph individuals. The connection between a photographer and their subject can be quite intimate. My models are sharing a side of themselves with me that they might not regularly share with everyone else.

So, what does consent look like in this context? Before working with my models, I always have a discussion with them about what the shoot may look like: the scenes that we may want to play out, possible poses, maybe the inclusion of additional models, and wardrobe (or lack thereof) options. It is important that we both agree on all these details before I ever snap the first photo.

Just because someone has given me consent to photograph them in an attractive, seductive, or sexualized manner, it does not mean that I have open consent from them to touch or shoot them in any way I want. For example, if a model allows me to photograph them nude or semi-nude, it does not mean that I am allowed to just walk up to them and touch/pose their body, adjust their bra or maybe their jock without asking. I must ask them if it is okay, and they must say yes. Otherwise, I keep my hands off.

I was asked to select photographs from my collection that speak to the themes of this book. When making my selections I thought about situations and environments in which consent is present and part of the conversation. From this, I came up with five thematic issues that often come up in my work: seduction, connection, intimacy, D/s (Dominant/submissive) relationships, and community.

I chose to include the photographs titled Seduction #1 and #2 because of their sexy and seductive nature. Seduction #1 portrays a woman casting a very seductive gaze into the camera and wearing very sexy lingerie. I strongly believe that people should be allowed to exude sexiness, wear something seductive, or express themselves in any sexualized manner without being subjected to nonconsensual harassment or behavior.

Seduction #2 can be perceived in many ways. The man wearing a jockstrap may very well be dressing down to be seductive toward the person behind him. He may have just thrown that jock on to feel sexy. But how did the touching/contact begin? Was there a discussion of consent before the two people began interacting? Or was it an unspoken and natural progression of actions that were welcomed by both? This photograph leaves much to the imagination.

Consent can foster deep connections. Consent is sexy. When you allow someone into your space or someone allows you into theirs, that invitation to openness can create a bond or an experience that is overwhelmingly erotic. Connections #1, #2, and #3 provide a glimpse into the kinds of experiences that consent allows people to explore.

Consent creates intimacy. Intimacy #1 portrays a very tender, soft moment between a Dom and her submissive. Intimacy #2 portrays a very similar moment. In D/s (Dominant/submissive) relationships, moments like this frequently follow an intense scene. In the community, these acts of intimacy are commonly referred to as "after care."

Submission #1, #2, #3, and #4 all provide a glimpse into the type of power exchange that can take place within D/s relationships. These relationships always start with negotiations and consent. Not only does the submissive need to consent to being dominated but the Dominant also has to give the submissive consent to touch them, serve them, or submit to them in any given context.

The importance of consent is woven throughout the Leather+Kink+Fetish community. Most players within the community will attest to the fact that it all begins with consent and that consent is fundamental. Community #1 simply portrays players within the community posing in a provocative manner. It is our responsibility as individuals and as a community to stress the importance of consent to foster healthy sexual relationships.

My photography work is very sexual in nature. But when I reflect on the work that I do within the Leather+Kink+Fetish community, I am not simply trying to capture images of sexualized individuals or content. Instead, my goal is to create a mood, a feeling, or a familiar situation that you might experience in real life. Because of this, ideas of consent often resonate deeply with the moments I capture with my camera.

Seduction #1.

Seduction #2.

Connections #1.

Connections #2.

Connections #3.

Intimacy #1.

Intimacy #2.

Submission #1.

Submission #2.

Submission #3.

Submission #4.

Community #1.

PART 2

Responding to Sexual Harm

8

Before Consent, after Harm

BLU BUCHANAN

Whether male, female, working or middle class, the first
direct sense of political power comes from the
apprehension of massed bodies.
—Samuel Delany, *The Motion of Light in Water*, 1988, p. 293

In many marginalized communities, the idea of a discrete individual sits uncomfortably alongside the ways we are connected to and care for one another. We are our ancestors, we are the people we fuck, we are someone else's dreams. And yet consent is generally understood as individual, interpersonal (between two or, less often, more individuals), transactional, and private. This framework lends itself to the neoliberal insistence on personal choice as our primary metric of freedom.[1] Understanding consent only as an exchange between individuals also translates social life into a legal frame that reduces our relationships to what is legible to our settler-colonial courts. The language of individual choice and personal preference shows up perhaps most obviously in our erotic lives within the context of online sexual racism on apps like Grindr, Scruff, Growlr, and Tinder, with explicitly structural biases found in comments like "no blacks, no fats, no femmes."[2] In less obvious ways, this neoliberal notion of consent has wiggled into our current mainstream conversations, which focus not on how systems of power produce harm but on a transactional, additive understanding of individual relationships of consent and harm.[3] Why do we often treat consent and harm in singular ways?

Before diving any further into the concept of community consent, it is important to situate myself as a scholar and community member. I approach this work as a light-skinned Black nonbinary femme and as a survivor of sexual violence, and I draw heavily in this chapter on my experiences of sexual harm and community healing. I am invested in the practice of abolition: abolition of capitalism, hierarchies of power, the prison system, trans antagonism, and global anti-Blackness. I write this for others who, like me, are attempting to develop a queer culture that is radically accountable while resisting the siren call of the carceral system within which we have been socialized.

Who can help us trace these alternative practices? For this I turn to Samuel Delany's memoir, *The Motion of Light on Water*, where he recounts his experience of first entering the St. Marks Baths in New York's East Village of the early 1960s.[4] Delany describes entering the multistory building "in which ponderous old men slept, wheezing and coughing," on the first floor; walking past the rooms with their doors open, "the men inside naked and ass up—in clear, if silent invitation" on the second; until he finally arrives on the third floor.[5] "In the gym-sized room were sixteen rows, four to a rank, or sixty-four altogether. I couldn't see any of the beds themselves, though, because there were three times that many people (maybe a hundred twenty-five) in the room. Perhaps a dozen of them were standing. The rest were an undulating mass of naked male bodies, spread wall to wall."[6] Delany goes on to describe both the fear that this initially evoked and how this scene differed from other forms of public sex: it was the scene's unbounded and unpartitioned nature that gave him a sense of political and social agency.

Drawing on Delany's figure of "massed bodies" through which we can imagine political power, my invitation is for us to reconsider consent as collective, relational, and public. To understand consent in this way, we must be attentive to the affective aspects of its operation. Affect, a preconscious force that creates connections between the body and the world, is the dark matter to which Delany gestures with his concept of "massed bodies."[7] This kind of affective mechanism of consent is already built into a particular, imperfect architecture within queer and kink spaces.

Unlike Delany's visual account of St. Marks, when I entered my first bathhouse I was struck first by the sounds and smells that filled the space. A thumping electronic set played by a DJ, with a BPM set to mimic a racing heart. The smell of chlorine, sex, and soap vied for dominance beneath an overwhelming layer of eucalyptus. In contrast to the often overly visual focus of queer men's spaces, this bathhouse downplayed the role of sight; after stepping past the brightly lit membership window and signing up for a locker, a room, or a premium suite, you steadily moved into dimmer and darker spaces the farther you explored.[8] Past the showers, the steam room, and sauna were rows of cubicle-like rooms. Past these rooms was a gym (appearances must be kept up, after all) and beyond that a maze-like series of hallways, platforms, and gloryholes.

Amid these sights, sounds, and smells another layer of signaling was added, different from the outside world. Long looks, head shakes, grazed hands, even the positioning of one's body took on meaning, communicating in rapid fire with each person you came across your interest in and consent to particular kinds of sexual activities. Even the wrist around which you chose to wear your locker key signaled your interest in a particular form of erotic play. Some enter the space knowing these rules. I, for example, had done copious research and had in-depth discussions with bathhouse regulars in preparation. Samuel Delany ended up at a bathhouse on a whim with some friends and entered completely without knowledge of how to navigate these spaces.[9]

By exploring in this chapter the bathhouse experiences of two Black queers, Delany and myself, I articulate how queer and kink communities create specific spatial relationships of consent and how they *might* respond ethically when the relational boundaries of their members are violated. Thus, what follows is split in two: what comes before and preempts our notions of individual consent, and what happens after members of the community have been harmed.[10]

Although the bathhouse has an ancient history, I focus on its manifestation in places like the United States in the twentieth and twenty-first centuries. There it has operated as a subversive space in which queer desires have been enacted, often, but not exclusively, among men.[11] In small, out-of-the-way corners of many major cities, you'll find small entrances to often vast and ponderous spaces with a multitude of different purposes. These spaces have frequently been raided, often shut down, and invariably targeted by local politicians intent on portraying a "tough on crime" stance to their voting blocs. That they are also sites of libidinal anonymity and socialization is not an accident.

That these spaces are erotic, public, and maintained by a set of rules that are understood but often go unspoken makes them ideal for talking about community forms of consent and their failures. Taking seriously the power of "massed bodies"—of consent within and beyond individual actors—we have to explore what it means to orient our sexual selves in public ways. Delany puts it best: "One might say, of course, that an orgy of three to five is one experience; and an orgy of a hundred or more is simply something very different, both materially and psychologically. To which I will counter that that is precisely the difference, at least psychologically, I am delineating."[12]

It is this delineation that I explore further in hopes that adapting community forms of consent and transforming them to better address our communal needs will be a form of resistance to the current neoliberal moment and the carceral logic involved in individual punishment.

What Comes Before

Ethnographer Robin Bauer found that, among queer BDSM practitioners, consent is the central feature distinguishing BDSM from violence or abuse.[13] Markedly different from nonqueer practitioners, these interviewees viewed consent as fundamentally informed by the social structures in which they live, rather than simply being a contractual relationship between two people. Consent for them is always partial, it requires work to maintain, and it must be practiced. Bauer calls it "negotiated consent" to distinguish it from the mainstream understanding of consent as a relationship between two people within a social vacuum.[14] This "negotiated" form of consent acknowledges the limits of the term, but it remains firmly understood as a process between individuals, rather than being produced by the "massed bodies" Delany describes when he first steps out into the open space of the bathhouse's third floor. I expand on the idea of negotiated consent as relational—not just between individuals but also between the community and its participants—as a generative way forward for building a culture of consent and accountability.

Consent produced by "massed bodies" is also predicated on negotiated consent but one that happens at the community rather than the individual level. Community, in this sense, is made up of people operating within a bounded social, geographic, or digital space who are held together by a shared sense of moral conduct and interdependency. This community consent does not negate the need for individual consent but transforms how and what consent looks like. Two visible, spatial differences between many queer kink and BDSM spaces and other sexual spaces are the bathhouse and the backroom. In both spaces, those entering are subject to the easing of some social rules and the imposition of new ones. These rules also shift as you range across the space. Moving between, as Delany puts it, the coughs of the first floor, the open invitations of the second, and the public play of the third means reorienting to different spatial and social rules.

These spaces run contrary to our general notion of consent because they do not rely on verbal affirmations: much of the cruising that happens in these spaces relies on the setting and on nonverbal communication to secure consensual engagement between participants. These spaces have rules to consent, although they are articulated in ways that, to an outsider, seem remarkably opaque. The concept of power, as reducible to the actions and choices of individuals, does not make sense within this queer architecture. Its presence is instead predicated on a shared knowledge and practice of the rules of cruising, the boundaries and signals that are supposed to be understood between all participants. It is an architecture oriented around and amenable to the political and sexual reality of "massed bodies."

But what happens when those signals are ignored, when the community rules that facilitate consensual participation between folks in the dim hallways, saunas, and showers fail?

One of my first forays into these spaces ended with my experiencing sexual violence, when someone was more interested in his own pleasure than my boundaries. The current structure of community consent falls short because of two overriding assumptions: all participants are knowledgeable of the rules of the space and how to engage (and disengage) with others, and breaches of consent are accidental rather than structural or interpersonal attacks. This leaves the space without any mechanism for (1) learning the rules or (2) addressing harm. Samuel Delany articulates how unsettled he felt on encountering the third floor of the bathhouse: he would be having an experience that he did not consent to because he did not know what to expect or how to navigate the space. This asks hard questions about how we can prefigure spaces like the bathhouse to address differences in power and address harm.

What Comes After

In the dark I could not see his face. Even if I had wanted to report him to the bathhouse staff, what kind of description could I give? My experience demonstrates why thinking about harm at the level of "massed bodies" is important, because it's only at that level that we can address community harm. My experience was personal, but it also represented a breakdown in the community consent process established for that space. Here is what comes after, after structures and interpersonal forms of consent break down.

How does transformative justice bear on the queer architecture of consent? How can this case help us see the potential for thinking queerly about healing and avoiding harm? The goal of transformative justice—which is integral to our reoriented definition of consent—is not to prevent all harm but to reduce it through structural interventions and to create pathways toward repair.[15] If harm spills over from the interaction of individuals, then addressing the harm between individuals leaves residues of harm: unaddressed stains that take community work to put right. Transformative justice is one way we can build on the practices of consent that we can already find in queer and kink communities.

Resisting neoliberal deployments of consent, community consent identifies nonconsensual encounters between actors as a breakdown and harm to the community as a whole. Thus, healing demands community-level acts to reorient structures of consent and redress harm. More explicit guidelines to negotiating spaces is one critical component, because understanding the rules and norms of the space can be intimidating and should not be taken for granted.[16] Helping people learn the rules of the space should also be part of our architecture of consent.

Simultaneously, we need to let go of the hetero- and homonormative stigma around public sexual spaces so we can facilitate the kinds of consent structures we deserve and to adjust them when they fail. The silence around public sexual spaces means that iterative mechanisms of crafting communal consent are often missing. Bathhouse goers should own their pleasure and their power within the sexual spaces we create and participate in. Sex panic keeps us from the structural, transformative work needed to make our spaces more ethical and consensual.

Unlike Delany, whose bathhouse experience ends with a return to the mundane world, my experience as a Black trans person was not so discrete. Amid the sexual and erotic tensions of this space, and the exhilarating experience of community consent, was the persistent question of whether, outside this space, these fellow travelers would do anything to make our in-bathhouse experiences more consensual. More bluntly, beyond the bathhouse, after we fuck, will they fight for me? Community consent requires us to do more work than checking in with our partners in the bedroom, the backroom, or other sexualized spaces. By shaping the affective atmosphere, the queer architecture of consent, it is possible for marginalized people to recast and remake those who refuse to dignify our lives outside the space.[17] To (very loosely) paraphrase Blaise Pascal's thoughts on religious practice, "I don't kneel to provide a blowjob because I care; I care because I kneel to provide a blowjob."[18] The space itself becomes transformational, it reorients meaning and shifts relationality, and in doing so it has the capacity to spill over and beyond the bathhouse itself. Thus, it demands participation in the dismantling of power structures, even as we practice and shift power between ourselves and those around us. Neoliberalism offers us an easier, if fundamentally more unsatisfying and unjust, answer.

Conclusion

Janelle Monáe says, "You fucked the world up now; we'll fuck it all back down."[19] Fucking it back down is an ongoing practice of envisioning our sexual and erotic relationships in ways that resist co-optation by systems that were never meant for marginalized peoples. So how can sex, paired with transformative justice, have an impact on the world? Power does not disappear. Its oppressive nature emerges from its power to dictate our language and the social world that language facilitates. As Bauer recognizes, power and consent are part of all aspects of our lives.[20] At the individual level that means that consent isn't only achieved by "matching" identities to erase power imbalances: it has to be negotiated and held by participants. On a community level it means using our structures of consent—the power of Delany's "massed bodies"—to accomplish the dismantling of power structures to achieve an ever-greater negotiated consent between individuals. Translating the power of "massed bodies" from the bathhouse to the "massed bodies" of direct action will harness the affective and social energy of the erotic.

Notes

1. Roderick A. Ferguson and Grace Kyungwon Hong, "The Sexual and Racial Contradictions of Neoliberalism," *Journal of Homosexuality* 59, no. 7 (2012): 1057–1064.

2. Brandon Andrew Robinson, "'Personal Preference' as the New Racism: Gay Desire and Racial Cleansing in Cyberspace," *Sociology of Race and Ethnicity* 1, no. 2 (2015): 317–330; Christopher T. Conner, "The Gay Gayze: Expressions of Inequality on Grindr," *Sociological Quarterly* 60, no. 3 (2019): 397–419; Damien Riggs, ed., *The Psychic Life of Racism in Gay Men's Communities* (Lanham, MD: Lexington Books, 2017).

3. See, for example, Jeremy Peters, "Alex Morse Was Accused, Condemned, then Vindicated. Will His Experience Change Anything?" *New York Times*, August 23, 2020.

4. Samuel R. Delany, *The Motion of Light in Water: Sex and Science Fiction Writing in the East Village* (Minneapolis: University of Minnesota Press, 1988).

5. Delany, *Motion of Light in Water*, 291.

6. Delany, *Motion of Light in Water*, 291.

7. Raymond Williams, *Marxism and Literature* (Oxford: Oxford University Press, 1977); Kristyn Gorton, "Theorizing Emotion and Affect: Feminist Engagements," *Feminist Theory* 8, no. 3 (2007): 333–348.

8. Lik Sam Chan, "Ambivalence in Networked Intimacy: Observations from Gay Men Using Mobile Dating Apps," *New Media & Society* 20, no. 7 (2017): 2566–2581; Courtney Blackwell, Jeremy Birnholtz, and Charles Abbott, "Seeing and Being Seen: Co-Situation and Impression Formation Using Grindr,

A Location-Aware Gay Dating App," *New Media & Society* 17, no. 7 (2014): 1117–1136.

9. Delany, *Motion of Light in Water*, 291

10. I define harm here in the same manner as adrienne marie brown, "Harm: the suffering, loss, pain, and impact that can occur both in conflict and in instances of abuse, as well as in misunderstandings steeped in differences of life experience, opinion, or needs," in *We Will Not Cancel Us* (Chino, CA: AK Press, 2020), 28.

11. Lauren Berlant and Michael Warner, "Sex in Public," *Critical Inquiry* 24, no. 2 (1998): 547–566; Allan Bérubé, "The History of Gay Bathhouses," *Journal of Homosexuality* 44, nos. 3–4 (2003): 33–53.

12. Delany, *Motion of Light in Water*, 293.

13. Robin Bauer, *Queer BDSM Intimacies: Critical Consent and Pushing Boundaries* (New York: Palgrave MacMillan, 2014), 76–77.

14. Bauer, *Queer BDSM Intimacies*, 79.

15. Mariame Kaba, *Creative Interventions Toolkit: A Practical Guide to Stop Interpersonal Violence*, https://www.creative-interventions .org/tools/toolkit; Mariame Kaba and Shira Hassan, *Fumbling towards Repair: A Workbook for Community Accountability Facilitators* (Chico, CA: AK Press, 2020).

16. Queer in the World, "Gay Sauna Etiquette: A Guide to the Perfect First Time Gay Sauna Experience," https://queerintheworld.com /gay-sauna-guide/.

17. Ben Anderson, "Affective Atmospheres," *Emotion, Space and Society* 2, no. 2 (2009): 7–81.

18. Blaise Pascal, *Pensées* (New York: Open Road, 2011). ProQuest Ebook Central, 83.

19. Janelle Monáe, "Screwed (ft. Zoë Kravitz)," Wondaland Productions, April 27, 2018, https://www.youtube.com/watch?v =fgSpeV-bklk.

20. Bauer, *Queer BDSM Intimacies*, 78.

9

Rejecting the (Black Fat) Body as Invitation

SHANTEL GABRIEAL BUGGS

It's 2019 and I'm out partying in New York City for the first time. With a drink in one hand, I hike up the hem of my maxi dress to simultaneously free up my legs while I grind on my dance partner and attempt to keep my clothes out of the alcohol and other unknown fluids on the cement dance floor. As the sweat and humidity pool on the floor and drip from the ceiling, as the multicolored lights flash and the bass thrums through my chest, as I smile at my friend/mentor/colleague across the room, the gay Black man behind me speaks in my ear loud enough to be heard over the music: "I don't fuck women but I'd take you home." I laugh, feeling strangely complimented. I joke with him and mention that I was only in town for a work conference and didn't have the time.

I feel amazed by the power my ass has to even turn out a gay man, though his seeming attraction to me isn't necessarily a new experience. This wasn't my first time being felt up and sexualized in a club, and it wasn't my first time having someone confess that I somehow had slipped past their typical preferences for sexual partners.

It's 2018 and I'm in a gay bar in Mexico. I'm sitting on a bar stool, drinking a beer after having danced to one of my favorite ass-shaking anthems. I look behind me and notice that two gay men are posing with their heads up against my ass, their friend gleefully taking pictures. Later, at another bar hosting a drag show, I dance on top of a raised platform and seemingly every cellphone in the room turns my way.

I can't decide if their fascination is with big asses or with Black people in general.

It's 2015 and its spring break in Austin, Texas. I am in a bar that I've frequented many times, celebrating my friend's admission to law school. She is downing the mason jar drinks that are the specialty of this bar (there's a reason they call them an Adios Motherfucker). I decide that one of us will need to be a bit sober to make sure we get home. A Black woman in baggy jeans and a sports jersey, with long false lashes and a thick, weave ponytail under a fitted baseball hat—what I grew up calling a stud but others might call an aggressive,[1] a butch, or a dyke—approaches us, focusing her attention on my friend. She grabs aggressively at my friend's waist and ass, pulling her toward her to dance. To draw attention away from my friend who is pretty drunk at this point, I slide in between them. Quickly, the stud's hands start roaming around my body. Several times, she shoves her hands into my loose palazzo pants to grab between my legs, and I scramble to pull them away. I can't remember if I told her to stop, but I know I tried to keep her hands away from me. I wanted to keep her away from my friend, and I also didn't know what other possible solution there was in this packed bar beyond letting her feel me up instead. Bodies were pressed together everywhere and the music was loud.

I didn't necessarily want her thrown out since she'd probably been drinking herself.

As she touched me, I kept having flashbacks to other nights in this same bar: men chasing me around on all fours trying to bite me on the ass, men caging me in up against the bar until I have a panic attack. I have endless stories of being touched without my permission in this bar, and yet I keep coming back.

It's 2011 and I'm in Lipstick, a lesbian bar in Austin. I'm dancing with my newly made graduate school friends, enjoying hanging out with a collective of queers. Suddenly, my head is yanked back due to an unseen hand that wrapped my hair around their forearm. I realize it was my friend, grinding up against my ass. I keep dancing even though it took me by surprise, and at no point had I mentioned that I might like my hair pulled or not.

I'm not upset but I also don't question why I'm *not* upset.

It's 2005 and I'm 18. I'm in the gay club in my hometown I've frequented with my two best friends, even though I hadn't fully admitted to myself that I was attracted to men *and* women. I would not identify as bisexual until after undergrad, when I was attending graduate school in Houston. At 18, I had a boyfriend who was two years older than me. Yet, I knew I loved being around queer folks. I knew I felt in community with them even if I wasn't "out." One night, I went to the gay club with my boyfriend (who was straight). I spent the night having gay men compliment my appearance and grope me flirtatiously. One man even picked me up off the ground aggressively in the middle of the dance floor, drawing my boyfriend's suspicious eye as I laughed awkwardly and struggled to be put down. Women also touched me unbidden, caressing or grabbing my breasts and commenting on how they wished they had big titties too.

Yet I can't recall feeling uncomfortable; I mean, my best friends used to comment on my breasts all the time too, poking me with pencils and marveling at how many sports bras I had to wear for any kind of physical exercise. It seems these early experiences set the tone for how I have approached being in certain spaces ever since—both those catering to queer communities and not.

As these memories demonstrate, nightclubs and bars are not just a place for fun and exploring intimacy with others. They're not just a place to pick up willing sexual or romantic partners. For people like me, they are also often a primary venue wherein our bodies are violated, are viewed as available for consumption. bell hooks argues that the "'real fun' is to be had by bringing to the surface all those 'nasty' unconscious fantasies and longings about contact with the Other."[2] I have experienced a lifetime of these racialized and gendered fantasies being projected on my body in these spaces in which alcohol and other substances lower inhibitions.

This essay contends with a double bind: the ways that as a Black queer woman I am sexualized, othered, and viewed as available, and the ways that I must navigate who is doing that fetishizing and whether I wish repercussions for the person(s) engaging in that behavior.[3] Here, I attempt to assess how I have denied justice and fair treatment to myself as a Black queer woman out of my concern for other queer people, because of the ways the social structures we live within target queer people and people of color for unequal and unjust treatment. How has my embodiment and past experiences informed how these moments shift from "genuine" desire to unwanted fetishizing? What does it mean that I do not (or feel that I cannot) protect myself as a queer person of color so that I can instead protect others? Why is this desire to protect a responsibility I feel compelled to take on? How can

I reject the perception that my body is an open invitation while also rejecting carceral logics?

A Body as Spectacle and as Invitation

I am a light-skinned multiracial Black bisexual woman with a fat but also fairly tall and hourglass-shaped body: I have big titties, big ass, and hips and thighs—and a belly too. With my body and big curly hair, I am consistently made a spectacle in nightclub spaces. In heteronormative bars, seemingly everyone, but especially straight men and women, feel entitled to my body.

Squirming through packed crowds is always an exercise in trying to avoid having my ass, waist, arms, or hair grabbed or caressed. I often stick to dancing with women because it is "safe," but their enthusiastic slaps of my ass, forceful grabbing of my hips, the insistence that we document this moment with photos (or, more likely, someone's smartphone flashing in the dark without my consent) make me question what safety really means.

In queer-designated spaces, I tend to lack the fears I may have elsewhere. However, this doesn't stop others from desiring me and expressing that desire or fascination by placing their hands on me.

I have struggled with what it means to consent to touching in nightclubs and bars. I want to assume that the alcohol loosened up other people and facilitated behavior they would not otherwise engage in. Blame it on the alcohol, right? I don't want to ruin their good time by calling security or a bouncer to kick them out. I don't want to ruin my own good time by fighting them and setting myself up to be kicked out or arrested.

An underlying fear is also how someone might react with violence if I respond negatively. Harassment from strangers is normalized in public spaces, especially when the harassers are cisgender, heterosexual men. (Heteronormative) sexual aggression in bar settings is considered appropriate and perhaps even *expected* because of the presence of alcohol and the misogynistic logics that permeate these spaces.[4] In my experience, this can be heightened in bars geared toward LGBTQ folks because of the common perception that folks are intentionally coming there looking for sex or romance.

Navigating Bodily Justice

I have agonized for years about how I accept that people will touch me aggressively in public. I feel pressure to not make waves because we are "just having fun"—and this pressure is significantly more acute when I am in queer spaces or am with queer people. On more than one occasion, I ignored or tolerated behavior by a queer person that I would never let a straight man get away with, because I do not want to risk repercussions for a person who is already structurally and socially marginalized. I internalized the idea that I should be open to this kind of attention from my fellow queers, because to reject it is to be a "bad" queer—much like the disjointedness Roxane Gay describes in her experiences of being a "bad feminist."[5]

I have been socialized by the persistent invasion of my personal space to tolerate these behaviors as the price of frequenting nightclubs and bars; in queer spaces, I am supposed to view it as a compliment.

Am I rejecting what Cathy Cohen and Tamara Jones call a "liberatory politics"[6] when I lump queer folks in with straight folks, when I don't necessarily enjoy the open and unabashed desire of my fat, racialized queer body? I am not sure. I agree with Cohen and Jones that heterosexism is a system of oppression intertwined with anti-Black racism and that this mutual construction prevents the affirmation of Black queer folks (and especially Black queer women) in Western society. However, in rejecting the overlapping oppressions of heterosexism and racism, do we leave room for our fellow queers to feel safe? To feel they can reasonably protect themselves when an encounter goes in a direction they do not desire, even if it is something as trivial as dancing in the club?

What do we do when the lines between invited and uninvited hands are blurred?

Researchers have argued that one strategy for reducing sexual harassment in the time of #MeToo is to encourage so-called upstanders—people who come forward to intervene or speak out against harassment.[7] Their intervention can be a means of avoiding the involvement of law enforcement and putting people into contact with the criminal "justice" system. However, although this upstanding is certainly appropriate for violent and egregious instances of harassment and assault, it does not provide guidance for responses to violations like those I described in the memories that open this essay. How to tell whether someone's dancing is a little too handsy or if the person being touched is uncomfortable? In being an upstander, do we set ourselves up to be another form of police?

That upstanding doesn't even seem to work in more serious scenarios is not lost on me; in cases like my own assault by two white straight men that occurred after a night out drinking and dancing at a bar with friends, my lack of consent was probably hard for outsiders to discern. I had flirted and danced with one of these men in the bar. I came home with my friend and her boyfriend at the time, my mind hazy and missing the parts of the evening after we left the bar (I threw a lot of syrup around at Waffle House, I learned the next day); but to everyone else I didn't seem out of it.

In the time my friend took a quick shower, her boyfriend's friends/roommates had taken me into their room. Perhaps, my friend's boyfriend should have been an "upstander" if he thought that I was not fully aware of what was happening (I can't remember if he said anything at all). His friends could have been upstanding, too.

I am not at fault that I could not more clearly convey that I was in no position to consent. The fault clearly lies with the men who did not even bother to ask. The fault lies with a society that assumes that an openly bisexual Black woman who flirts is always open to sex.[8]

I can intervene on my own or others' behalf in the bars, but then I also run the risk of being labeled a "prude." The convoluted combination of my anticarceral politics and a lifetime of normalization of bodily accessibility sets me up to sacrifice my own feelings of safety and autonomy to maintain the safety of others.

We must develop other means of keeping our communities safe while maintaining practices and norms that reject heteronormativity and avoid putting a damper on the intimacy and exhilaration that dancing in a nightclub can produce. A commitment to bodily autonomy means that, in addition to supporting bodily integrity and sexual freedom, we also commit to racial and gender justice. This commitment requires us to rethink how our communities may reinforce the racist and sexist socialization that queer people of color receive. Is it possible to create spaces wherein we willingly share our bodies with others or take pleasure from the seeming violation and fetishization of our bodies while also rejecting the perpetuation of logics that lead queer folks to believe they *must* allow their bodies to be accessible? I believe it is. We have an obligation to reject the bad queer as a specter, haunting our interactions and creating opportunities for fear—of rejection, of expulsion from our communities—to inform our behavior. We must do the internal work to evaluate our racist and sexist biases. I hope for a world where we can not only enjoy ourselves freely but also make no expectations of others or demand more than they want to give.

Notes

1. An "aggressive" or "AG" is a woman with a masculine gender presentation. It is a genderqueer discourse rooted in Black class and masculinity, as well as prison culture. To read more, see Kara Keeling, "Looking for M—: Queer Temporality, Black Political Possibility, and Poetry from the Future." *GLQ* 15, no. 4 (2009): 565–582.

2. See bell hooks, "Eating the Other: Desire and Resistance," in *Black Looks: Race and Representation* (Boston: South End Press, 1992), 21–39.

3. The "double bind" has been used to name a variety of phenomena, from the double-bind theory of schizophrenia—wherein contradictory communication between family members serves as a form of control—to naming the sexual double standard for heterosexual women that constrains the articulation of desire. Here, I am describing something perhaps more akin to double consciousness, wherein my positionality and politics create internal conflict and constrain how I respond to harms. See Gregory Bateson, Don D. Jackson, Jay Haley, and John Weakland, "Toward a Theory of Schizophrenia," *Behavioral Science* 1, no. 4 (1956): 251–264; Charlene L. Muehlenhard and Marcia L. McCoy, "Double Standard/Double Bind," *Psychology of Women Quarterly* 15, no. 3 (1991): 447–461; W. E. B. Du Bois, *The Souls of Black Folk* (Chicago: A. C. McClurg & Co., 1903).

4. College men self-report engaging in sexually aggressive behavior in drinking settings, citing these behaviors as a means of demonstrating assertiveness and the willingness to take risks. See Edward H. Thompson Jr. and Elizabeth J. Cracco, "Sexual

Aggression in Bars: What College Men Can Normalize,"
Journal of Men's Studies 16, no. 1 (2008): 82–96.

5. Roxane Gay, *Bad Feminist: Essays* (New York: Harper Collins, 2014).

6. Cathy J. Cohen and Tamara Jones, "Fighting Homophobia versus Challenging Heterosexism: 'The Failure to Transform' Revisited" in *Dangerous Liaisons: Blacks, Gays, and the Struggle for Equality* (New York: New Press, 1999), 80–101.

7. See, for more, Kristen Renwick Monroe, "Ending Sexual Harassment: Protecting the Progress of #MeToo," *Journal of Women, Politics & Policy* 40, no. 1 (2019); 131–147.

8. Let's not even get into the number of messages I get on dating apps from couples who assume I'll be open to threesomes with them simply because I am bisexual.

10

My Firsts

On Gaysian Sexual Ethics

JAMES McMASTER

They say you never forget your first love. There's a reason for that. When you first find yourself taken with another, you're taken by surprise. So, when you fall for them you free-fall and usually to the bottom of adolescence's hormonal wishing well. You don't go in guarded because you don't know that falling in love is a thing to guard against, at least not at first. And this is especially true when you're queer: no one tells you that the feelings you feel for your best friend might be more than the feelings of friendship. You have to parse the pain to figure that out, and the trauma of this first romantic drama will coauthor your love stories for the rest of your life. What I'm saying is: you never forget your first love because, in a manner of speaking, and if you're lucky, your first love is also your first nonconsensual sensual relation. Mine was, and it wasn't my last either.

What you're reading is my attempt to grapple with this fact in the form of what Andrea Long Chu calls a "coincidence report."[1] Unlike an incident report, which is a series of putative facts legitimated by the cops after a crime, the genre of the coincidence report attempts to cobble together, aesthetically and affectively, an event—in this case, events—whose ontological status is unstable even for those who experienced it. Was that person being racist to me, or was I just being oversensitive? Was the kiss we shared ethical? Was the sex we had? I'm not talking about differences of opinion between two parties involved in an encounter; I'm talking about sincere uncertainty. Maybe by the end of this report we'll be closer to knowing the difference.

I won't tell you the name of my first love, but I will tell you these three things: he was my best friend, he insisted he was straight, and the way I loved him hurt like nothing in my life has hurt since. Teenager that I was, though, I didn't know I'd fallen for him at the time—not for certain. What I knew was that my desires were at war with each other. On one side, the desire to be normal made its last stand from a foxhole dug by the promises of state recognition, family acceptance, biological children, and privilege, pure and simple—being Asian in America was hard enough already, I thought. On the other side of the war, the stronger side, the desire to touch and to be touched by this beautiful boy marched unstoppably over the battlegrounds of my mind.

One autumn day, the beginning of the end for my first love and me, we sat in his parents' driveway, my car providing our only privacy. He spoke first: "What do you need from me?" A moment passed; it felt long. "I need you to kiss me," I said. If I'm being honest, dear reader, I didn't *need* him to kiss me to know how *I* felt; I *wanted* him to kiss me to know how *that* felt. A question for my fellow former closet cases, those who know what it is to search a not-quite-queer body for answers about ourselves: What is the difference between experimentation and instrumentalization? Even then I knew that I was using this boy the way a mountain climber—exhausted and exploring unknown, harrowing heights—might use a rope to pull themself to a new plateau. He was my lifeline and I loved him, but he was also a means to an end. And what do I owe him for that? My gratitude? An apology? Something more severe?

After a long pause, with hands held and eyes closed, we kissed. It was as fleeting as it was infinite.

We were two lonely brown boys just trying to survive the small minds of a small town where the racism (surprise, surprise) was constant. I played soccer growing up, and the only other Filipino boy in my town was on my team. Whenever I had the ball, white parents screamed his name. Whenever he had the ball, they cheered for me. No one ever apologized or tried to learn the difference.

Call it a trauma bond or call it a friendship, but what I had with my first love was my only sanctuary from all of this structural stupid. That is, until the armies of my desire arrived to raze our relationship to the ground. Overwhelmed by wanton want, I eventually told him, "It hurts too much to be your friend." His reply felt like a lie, but I let it be true because I so badly wanted to: "What if I said that we should be more?" What followed were flashes of something just short of sex: mouths met moments that were once just fantasies; hands held tight to things that seemed too good to be true. And were they? Was he expressing a queer impulse even more impossible than my own, or was he simply so in need of a friend that he would give his desires over as hostages to mine? I still don't know the answer to this question, but I do know how much that answer matters. In the former scenario we're two closeted kids, caught in a hurricane of heteronormativity, desperately trying together to get to shelter. In the latter, I'm wearing a ski mask over my face as I hold our friendship like a handgun to the back of this boy's head demanding whatever I can get from the bank vault of his body.

I probably don't have to tell you that whatever we had between us didn't last. In my late twenties I would find my first love on Facebook and send him a message apologizing "for everything." When he wrote back he said, "We were kids." It wasn't absolution, but it was enough.

Months after the end of my first love affair I fled to college—a small liberal arts school in Pennsylvania's third-largest city. It was the kind of place where the children of New York City's suburbs gathered to learn about their white privilege while the rest of us watched, took notes, and planned our next move. My first lesson of this sort came not weeks into my first semester, when I gave what was left of my gay virginity to the first cute-enough white boy that would let me call him "boyfriend." We did it in his basement dorm room, and by "it" I mean . . . well, something. I remember wanting very badly to get all the below-the-belt stuff under my belt; I needed to be finished with firsts. So, bluntly, we took turns getting fucked. It felt like pain and pooping, and we announced as much to one another as it was happening. It was his first time too. Looking back, we could have used a little more lube and a lot more sex education. Still, it was fun to be wanted by whiteness like I'd never been before. And the sex was fun too—like how failing to backstroke across ball pits used to be. I never imagined that my sexual fantasies would be less fantastic in reality until I actually tried to realize them, you know?

Sometimes—as in your first time(s)—you don't know you have a boundary until you've already passed it. A move gets made, a line gets crossed, and you find yourself standing with someone else in territories ranging from uncomfortable to unsafe. What should happen then?

A year or so after that first fuck, my first boyfriend, now my first ex-boyfriend, would offer his help when noticing me drunkenly stumbling to the bathroom at a party. When we got there, he stood behind me as I stood over the toilet and vomited. I was tasting stomach acid and shame when it happened. I felt his hands unbuttoning my jeans, his fingers feeling around beneath my boxers. I didn't say no (I was throwing up . . .), but I did struggle to remove his hands from my pants. He persisted, though, and I, barely able to hold my head up, stopped struggling.

When my stomach finally emptied, I turned to face him, but before I could wipe my mouth clean and my eyes clear he kissed me on the lips and forced his tongue against mine. After a few suffocating seconds I pushed myself free and hobbled back into the party.

It might surprise you, but I didn't think much of it at the time. It didn't feel violent; it felt annoying and even arousing. He was probably horny and one drink away from where I was. It was stupid, sloppy seduction from someone I used to know—a forgivable crime.

I didn't second-guess his actions until the next morning when he texted me an avalanche of apology. Surging, heavy, cold. "Please don't say anything." "It will never happen again." "I'm so sorry." Like many men before him, his apology was also a confession. And he, it seemed, was just a cliché.

Despite this, however, I didn't want to file a formal complaint. Partially this was practical: I had no desire, as Sara Ahmed might put it, to become a problem by exposing a problem.[2] Mostly, though, I didn't want to press charges because I didn't think that what happened was that bad. Assaulted or not, I felt unscathed and unharmed by most of what straight scripts teach us to fear from sexual violence (pitiless penetration, possible pregnancy, etc.). And if my assailant's fondling became something more forceful, if push came to shove, I liked my odds in that fight. It might be that, as a cis gay dude, I was somewhat insulated from the evils a straight woman might face in similar circumstances. It might also be that, lacking queer models against which to measure my experience of sexual violence, the event of my assault could never crystallize for me as such, leaving me less inclined, some might say, to recognize what I'd been through for what it was. While those who would say such a thing might be right, I bet those same people would also say that it's my right to narrate my own experience and to have that narration respected as truth. So, I didn't (and still don't) think the impact of my first ex's actions warranted the consequences he might (but likely wouldn't) have faced had I accused him of what he had done. And, as a good abolitionist, I didn't much believe in that kind of punitive consequence anyway.

Sometimes a boundary you know you have (or should have) is crossed, but you find yourself feeling, like, fine or whatever. What should happen then?

Before you answer I should tell you that I'm not the only gaysian I know with a story to tell—an incriminating one—about my ex-boyfriend. And all the stories follow a similar pattern: he pursued us, first sexually and then romantically, and, desire-starved Asian boys that we were, we let him. Some of us dated him, others only entertained the idea, but whatever the case we all were left with sexual scars that we'd show one another at parties as if to say, "no big deal," as if to say "me too" before #MeToo became a movement hell-bent on reminding the world that rape didn't have to be a rite of passage for certain sexually subordinated subjects. Back then, we couldn't speak of ourselves as survivors of assault, at least not to one another. #Metoo meant something more (or less?) than survivorhood. It meant membership in the most fucked up fraternity. We were pledge brothers bound by a sexual hazing ritual, keepers of an open secret that we had each learned the hard way. Duty-bound by racial inheritance, it became our responsibility to pass this information along to anyone who reminded us of our younger, more innocent selves. This, we must have thought, was just what it meant to be a brown boy in a world ruled by rice queens.[3]

I know better now. Between 2017 and 2019, I served as co-political chair for GAPIMNY, a volunteer-based organization in New York City dedicated to empowering and politicizing queer Asians. During those years I would regularly attend the happy hours that GAPIMNY's social committee would host every other Friday in a Hell's Kitchen gay bar. GAPIMNY calls these happy hours "Elixir." You should know that I owe Elixir many of the best parts of my life. It's where I learned to want folks like me. It's where I found my partner and so many of my people. And still, in my experience, it is also a space filled with racial inequalities and sexual ambiguities.

I would say that the majority of the happy hour's attendees come in search of the kind of sexual solidarity that Cynthia Wu and Nguyen Tan Hoang see in "sticky rice" relations between Asian men. I count myself in this category, and by now you should understand why. After spending so much of my life carried away in decidedly whitewater rapids—tossed from the raft of racial privilege, drowning in my desire to be desired—it's hard for me to see what Wu calls the "world making" project of sticky solidarity, of Asian men loving Asian men, as anything other than something lifesaving, a safe shore on which to take in, as if for the first time, the fresh breath of mutual recognition.[4] But not everyone at Elixir feels the way I do. Rice queens, usually both white and wealthy, attend the happy hour expecting attention, flirtation, and, in their own way, community. That they aren't invited never seems to faze them because, indeed, there are always ample gaysians—some might say "potato queens"—competing for the white gaze of the white gays, no matter how mediocre their politics or personalities might be. This fact, of course, angers the sticky rice gaysians whose dating pools are already too shallow. And they have a right to be angry, I think, so long as they aim that anger either at the intrusive whites or the sociopolitical situation. But blaming one another for desires that we often can't control, as so many often do, won't get us anywhere. Neither will focusing so intensely on how race rules our romantic lives that we miss how other forms of difference—gender expression, (dis)ability, fatness, class, even ethnicity—make it more or less possible to cuddle or kiss our crushes on any given night. Sticky rice world-making should not be about the "legislation of desire," to borrow Nguyen's words of warning.[5] We are not senators of a gaysian body whose task is to tell people whom they can and cannot fuck. What we are is full of desire to be valued for what we're worth, by ourselves and others, despite all these dynamics, which make up the libidinal economy of the urban gaysian scene. None of us consent to this unjust distribution of desire and desirability, but we are in it together, feeling our way through—literally.

Consider this: I'm at Elixir and another gaysian wraps his arms around me. I don't consent to this, but they seem tipsy, friendly, and harmless enough so I giggle and wiggle away. That same night, someone—I don't see who—grabs my ass. This act in a straight bar might cross a line, but does it here? Does the race of the grabber matter? Does the fact that I was more flattered than offended make it okay? I suspect a lot of queers would say that we have to let go of hard-and-fast rules and acknowledge that we each draw our boundaries differently. But, of course, that's just as tricky. If a super-hot stranger kissed me goodbye on the lips, I might love it; but honestly, if a not so hot stranger did the same, No, thank you. So, are the conventionally pretty privileged less likely to transgress? That's not a world I want to live in—though, of course, I already do—and this is to say nothing about what happens when new hands find involuntary hard-ons on a dance floor, or when some extra-extroverted someone backs into you at a sex party and you find yourself—surprise!—inside of them. Is that somehow not the unwanted sexual contact referenced in New York's legal definition of sexual abuse? (I'm asking earnestly, not rhetorically.) Is this just the price we have to pay to play?

I doubt it and I have some questions. When does the queer Asian context provide for pleasures unknown to the straight white world, and when does it cause us to confuse sexual misconduct for something else: closeted boys being boys, a rite of passage, a sloppy seduction, or a heretofore beloved form of non-normative intimacy?

My point: the scripts of straight white sexual ethics fit queer Asians like the baseball gloves we never wanted. We don't throw and catch on the same field, in the same way, or by the same rules. We may not throw or catch at all. Of course, many queer subcultures have ethically sound sexual scripts, and, even when they don't, sex without a script isn't always a bad thing. The question, though, is this: How do we know for sure when it is?

Notes

1. Andrea Long Chu, "Study in Blue: Trauma, Affect, Event," *Women & Performance: A Journal of Feminist Theory* 27, no. 3 (2017): 303.

2. See Sara Ahmed, *Living a Feminist Life* (Durham, NC: Duke University Press, 2017).

3. For more on the Asian man/white man dyad, see Eng-Beng Lim, *Brown Boys and Rice Queens: Spellbinding Performance in the Asias* (New York: New York University Press, 2013).

4. Cynthia Wu, *Sticky Rice: A Politics of Intraracial Desire* (Philadelphia: Temple University Press, 2018), 1.

5. Nguyen Tan Hoang, *A View from the Bottom: Asian American Masculinity and Sexual Representation* (Durham, NC: Duke University Press, 2014), 176.

11

Was I a Teenage Sexual Predator?

MARK S. KING

We were on a dirt road in the cotton fields, sitting in the back of his Plymouth. It had been my idea to stop and look at the sky, and I didn't think it came off as a sneaky move on my part, because the moon was full and bright and gorgeous.

I had been making small talk, which felt stupid, and I wished he would hurry up and make his move. This was the part that was always kind of boring. He was nice, though, and good-looking, maybe around 35.

It was a balmy Louisiana night in 1975. And I was a 14-year-old boy.

Everything went as planned, and he got me home on time so no one suspected. But he was a lot more nervous about it than I was.

And that was the routine during my teenage years. I had given up trying to seduce other boys my age because it took forever to talk them into anything and I didn't want them to freak out about it. So, I got involved in community theater productions during the summer, playing bit parts or working the spotlight, just to be in the company of gay men. Then it was just a matter of getting some time alone with them.

My strategy worked with some regularity, and it never occurred to me there might be something inappropriate or perverse or even criminal about it. At least, it never occurred to *me*.

People tell me that the criminal ramifications most certainly occurred to *them*. They say I was molested or abused and that the sex between us was the very definition of the word "statutory." They say I was dealing with adults who had the capacity to know better. And, most bruising to my ego, they tell me that my seductive charms were irrelevant and that perhaps it was the grown men who were doing the manipulating.

I wonder if my teenage memories are trustworthy and whether my furtive machinations set the stage for adulthood in ways I've failed to comprehend. Before I became a man, before the failed relationships and the sexual compulsions and the multiple drug addictions, I was a teenager who took dangerous walks alone in public parks and got into strange cars and suggested we drive somewhere more private.

What was I pursuing exactly, and did it ruin me? Was my fate sealed in the cotton fields of Louisiana?

My therapists believe it was, at least when they have been willing to discuss the matter at all. At the mere mention of my sexual behaviors as an adolescent, more than one counselor has interrupted my story to state that they were obligated to report any incidents of childhood sexual abuse. Even if the perpetrators were dead.

I felt abandoned by those mental health professionals, left to my own confusion and coping devices. I know that, on paper, my battles with addiction and my checkered relationship history form a textbook case of the wreckage caused by childhood sexual abuse. But that was also a typical journey for many a gay man coming of age, searching for validation for our burgeoning homosexuality and finding solace in the company of whoever would have us.

I don't feel damaged by those men, despite the facts of my life trajectory. The men I coaxed to those dusty roads aren't villainous to me. I can't bring myself to reduce them to simple pathology.

From the inside looking out, my teenage self was getting exactly what he wanted. My youthful yearnings can easily be compartmentalized—until I look at a 14-year-old boy today and am horrified at the very thought of him being preyed on. The compartment is shattered, and then, for some reason, I immediately work to rebuild it.

I met Jim in August, right before my freshman year in high school. The summer community theater musical was *1776*, and I was a stagehand. It was a cast made up almost entirely of men, many of whom were gay. Jim wasn't my first target.

After a matinee performance one afternoon, I asked him for a ride to a pool party that someone was throwing for the cast and crew. Once inside his car, I told him I forgot my bathing suit and asked if we could stop at his place so I could borrow one. What followed was a pitiful, half-naked fashion show in his bedroom and a brief, awkward encounter between us.

Afterward, I happily got back in the car, but Jim wasn't talking much. He had become really quiet as soon as we were done.

We had driven only a few blocks when Jim let out a kind of cough, like he was trying to stifle something and it burst out anyway. I looked over, and his whole face was wet.

"What's wrong?" I asked. I had seen men in very personal situations, but I had never seen one cry.

He pulled the car over and turned it off. Suddenly, everything felt quiet and important.

"What is it?" I asked in a careful voice. "Am I in trouble?"

He was searching the car console for something and found a packet of Kleenex. He held it in his lap and started to speak while he opened it.

"I'm twice your age, Mark," he said into his lap. His eyes were little cups of water, spilling. He turned to me. "You're 14 years old. I'm twice your age. Twice."

His arithmetic meant nothing to me. His expression toward me, sad and quizzical, felt like he was trying to read my mind. It made me uncomfortable. I didn't know what he wanted. I sat there and said nothing.

He turned away and gulped back more tears. And then he asked the most mysterious question of all. "Don't you . . . just want to be 14, Mark?"

I had no idea what the man was talking about. I sat staring at him with my mouth open. I was completely stumped. Seconds went by, and the car was silent.

My confusion seemed to disappoint him, because he shook his head slowly and looked back out the window. He was still very upset.

He wasn't simply crying out of guilt, they tell me now. They insist he was deflecting his own criminal behavior by blaming me for not acting my age. They tell me that he was the one who had trapped me and I didn't even know it.

Either way, I think Jim got more than he bargained for. I think he was a little frightened by the manipulative and unemotional 14-year-old sitting in his car that afternoon. And I think it saddened him because he cared about me.

And yes, I felt trapped all right, if only because I felt trapped in his car in this moment where things were not going as planned, because after ten minutes we were still parked on the side of the road and Jim wouldn't stop crying. I was staring at my shoelaces because I couldn't imagine a grown guy would want anyone to see him like this. He must be so embarrassed, I thought to myself. And I wished he would start the car, because the party was going on and there were probably lots of people having fun around the pool, and I really wanted to be there.

I finally looked over at Jim, and he was blowing his nose. Maybe that means we'll get moving again, I thought. Jim didn't say anything else, but he did finally turn on the ignition and the car rumbled to a start.

I was so relieved. I really wanted to see what was happening at the party.

That roadside scene happened more than forty years ago. I might say that it doesn't matter anymore or even tell myself that it never did. But to conjure up this story again, and then read my own words here, is to see myself as a young man, hardly more than a boy, who didn't possess the emotional capacity to understand why Jim was so upset, much less the meaning of what we had done.

Plenty of gay friends have tried to calm my mixed emotions by sharing their own youthful sexual adventures with adults. Other gay men have described sexual abuse to me, and when they speak of it their scars rise to the surface.

I don't feel scarred. It was youthful sport, most of the time. My consent was a given. I spent time and effort finding those partners. I understood what it was I wanted. I sought out men because I figured they would be less troublesome than boys my age. The fact they could have faced serious consequences didn't rob me of my consent to do it.

I am still puzzled by it all, still unsure whether I belong in the group of adventurers or with the abused. I can't seem to locate my own feelings. I have no judgment or anger or regret or shame. I don't feel much of anything about it.

That might be the most troubling thing of all.

12

(Trans)forming #MeToo

On Freedom for the "Unbelievable" Survivors of Gender Violence

V. JO HSU

"Our Constitution does not allow for cruel and unusual punishment. If it did, I have to say, I might allow what he did to
all of these beautiful souls—these young women in their
childhood—I would allow someone or many people to do to
him what he did to others."[1] These were the words of Judge
Rosemarie Aquilina when she sentenced Larry Nassar, the
USA Gymnastics doctor who assaulted hundreds of women
and girls in his care. For her ferocity, Aquilina was widely
celebrated as a champion of the #MeToo movement, meting
out justice in a limited legal system.[2] Although some critics
expressed unease with Aquilina's declarations, most did so
out of concern that she had violated judicial impartiality.
Missing from this conversation, as well as mainstream iter-
ations of #MeToo, was an interrogation of the criminal justice system as itself a perpetrator of gender-based violence.
Aquilina's statement alludes to the fact that prisons are a

presumed site of sexual and interpersonal violence. In fact, Nassar was attacked within hours of joining the general population of his Arizona penitentiary. The U.S. prison system is an institution that punishes through cruelty, and the forms of "justice" it enacts for survivors of sexual assault rely on the same disciplinary logics that enabled their trauma.

This chapter begins with the understanding that policing and prisons were designed to elicit obedience under white heteropatriarchal governance and that they continue to target people of color, disabled people, transgender and queer folks, and particularly those who live at the intersections of those identities. Any justice found in the judicial system will rely on the mechanisms used to enforce racialized gender hierarchies. Looking instead to grassroots organizations that defend incarcerated survivors of sexual and physical assault, I pursue alternative pathways to healing. These campaigns, built around queer and trans people of color (QTPOC) and women of color, necessarily respond to survivors' needs without turning to carceral solutions. Any future that protects transgender and queer people from targeted violence, I argue, must follow resonant frameworks—ones built by and in support of those historically abused by our social and state arrangements. Working toward such futures will necessitate an appreciation of how race, gender, and sexuality entwine to reify white heteropatriarchy. Trans and queer liberation, in other words, are inextricably bound to racial justice.

Race, Gender, and (Anti-)Carceral Logics

It is no accident that the most visible #MeToo cases involved Hollywood stars and champion athletes—survivors more readily legible to the public as "believable" targets of sexual assault. Blockbuster trials such as those of Harvey Weinstein and Larry Nassar relied on the testimonies of prominent, conventionally attractive, cisgender, heterosexual white women. These cases followed a storyline endemic to most popular media: a harm is done; legal authorities capture the perpetrator; the perpetrator is tried, found guilty, and locked away. This story assumes that the criminal legal system is (1) a trusted arbiter of "good" and "bad," (2) a means of redressing interpersonal harm, and (3) equally effective in responding to the pain of all survivors. As Judge Aquilina hints in her remarks to Nassar, however, the criminal justice system is notoriously a site of rape and sexual assault—and has historically inflicted that violence on trans and queer people and people of color.

Aquilina's wish that she could "allow" many people to "do to [Nassar] what he did to others" builds from the common knowledge that rape is intrinsic to prisons. To quote Gerard Bryant, a member of the New York City Board of Correction, "As long as we are going to have prisons, we are going to have sexual abuse in prisons."[3] A former associate warden, Bryant was likely unsurprised by the 2016 findings that 70 percent of sexual assault reports at Riker's Island involved jail staff.[4] Given that rates of incarceration for LGBTQ folks are many times higher than those of cisgender and heterosexual people,[5] and considering the racist past and present of policing,[6] prisons are an inevitable site of abuse for LGBTQ folks, particularly LGBTQ people of color.

Bryant's flippancy aside, he identifies the paradox at the heart of #MeToo: the carceral procedures through which it claims many of its victories are inseparable from rape culture. As historians and activists have long proven, police and prisons are extensions of the slavery on which this country was built—a system of domination where rape and sexual abuse are integral to assertions of power and control. By permitting enslavement "as punishment for a crime," the Thirteenth Amendment left a legal loophole that encouraged the criminalization and exploitation of Black folks. In our era of color-evasive racism, penal institutions conspire with discriminatory financial, housing, educational, and other social structures to place Black, Indigenous, trans, queer, disabled, undocumented, and other marginalized folks at greater risk of abuse—both interpersonal and state sanctioned.[7]

Within these legislated means of subjection, white gender norms undergird metrics for determining criminality. Black women and girls are frequently punished for violating the strictures of white femininity.[8] Black men and boys are portrayed as emasculated or hyperaggressive and threatening.[9] By the dictates of white heteropatriarchy, LGBTQ+ folks and Black LGBTQ+ folks in particular are regarded as deviant.[10] Given their uneven vulnerability to family rejection and workplace harassment, trans and queer folks are also more likely to wind up in underground economies. These social forces conspire to mark people of color, specifically trans and queer Black and Indigenous people of color (BIPOC), as already disorderly, threatening, or otherwise in need of containment, thereby creating a social and legal environment where they are more likely to be treated as criminal than victim.

Rejecting the presumed authority of the criminal legal system, this chapter builds from the experiential knowledge of trans and queer people and women of color who have been failed by U.S. courts and prisons. I focus on the work of three organizations—Survived and Punished (S&P), Love and Protect (L&P), and Freedom Overground—that defend criminalized survivors of gender violence. The cases that I examine demonstrate how stereotypes surrounding Black, trans, and/or lesbian identities obfuscate particular experiences of harm. Because S&P, L&P, and Freedom Overground start with the needs of those ignored or persecuted by the penal system, they necessarily envision forms of redress that do not require incarceration. Their work then models one of the founding principles of intersectional feminism: compassionate and *effective* solutions to damaging systems must be guided by the insights of those most vulnerable to their harms.[11] Importantly, this principle informed #MeToo's original conceptualization by activist Tarana Burke, who continues to center the experiences of Black women and girls and their healing.[12] For trans and queer folks working to address the staggering rates of sexual violence targeting our communities—inflicted from both within and without— these principles provide critical grounding for pursuits of gender justice.

#SurvivedandPunished: Against the Politics of Victimhood

In *#SurvivedandPunished: Survivor Defense as Abolitionist Praxis*, S&P and L&P draw from their experiences advocating for criminalized survivors to provide a "collection of tools, tips, lessons, and resources" for combating gender violence *and* the carceral systems that sustain it.[13] This online collection begins with a full-color, twenty-nine-page PDF, but the extensive use of hyperlinks locates its discussion within a constellation of other guides, essay collections, websites, campaign archives, social media, and other educational materials. On the first page, Alisa Bierria and coauthors inform readers that nearly 60 percent of people in women's prisons nationwide and as many as 95 percent of women in some prisons experience physical or sexual abuse prior to incarceration.[14] Among their examples are people such as Marissa Alexander, whom the prosecutor framed as an "angry Black woman" when he tried her for firing a warning shot at her abusive estranged husband.[15] She was using a registered gun, and the shot didn't harm anyone, but she was still sentenced to a mandatory minimum of twenty years for aggravated assault. Throughout their campaigns, Alexander's advocates pointed to how racialized gender stereotypes enabled the prosecutor to discredit and eventually blame Alexander for her own abuse.

Those same stereotypes became entwined with homophobia in the experiences of the "New Jersey 4": young Black lesbians who were targeted by misogynistic, homophobic, and racist sexual violence. When they defended themselves against an attack in a gentrified neighborhood, the prosecutors and the media framed them as a "killer lesbian gang."[16] Their assailant, Dwayne Buckle, threatened to "rape the young women 'straight."[17] After the ensuing fight, however, he claimed that he was "the victim of a hate crime against a straight man."[18] Media outlets throughout the country portrayed the four as a "wolf pack," playing on narratives of predatory lesbians and, again, angry Black women.[19] The four were sent to Riker's Island with sentences ranging from three and a half to eleven years. In the following years, Riker's Island was investigated and widely criticized for human rights abuses, including rampant sexual assault.

A few years after the sentencing of the New Jersey 4, Ky Peterson also collided with enforcers of racism and hetero- and cis-normativity. A Black trans man, Peterson was imprisoned for defending himself from a brutal physical and sexual assault.[20] Though the rape kit corroborated Peterson's story, the police insisted that he did not seem like a "believable victim" of rape.[21] Peterson's public defender encouraged him to sign a plea deal, insisting that self-defense was not a viable claim because Peterson is Black and "looks stereotypically gay."[22] The "deal" gave Peterson twenty years in prison, of which he served nine years before being released.

In each of these cases, prosecutors tapped into extant racialized gender stereotypes not only to censure but also actively criminalize the survivors. As Peterson's story in particular reveals, criminal cases are too often shaped by dominant assumptions about who constitutes a "believable victim" and a perpetrator. In the most widely circulated accounts of #MeToo, the survivors are white, affluent, conventionally attractive, cisgender, and heterosexual women. These cases illustrate how the very same scripts that presume the victimhood of white women also criminalize women of color, queer and transgender people, and anyone else who does not meet the bodily and behavioral expectations of white respectability.

Transformative Justice and Creating the Conditions for Freedom

In the *#SurvivedandPunished* toolkit, the authors trace the mistreatment of each survivor to injustices deeply embedded in the criminal legal system. For example, they point to how Alexander and Peterson were both denied Stand Your Ground immunity around the same time that Stand Your Ground helped acquit George Zimmerman for the murder of a Black teenager, Trayvon Martin. They offer further reflections on legislated discrimination with a reproduction of a Free Marissa Now poster. Beneath an illustration of Alexander's face, the text reads, "Stop the legal lynching of a Black domestic violence survivor by Florida's racist mandatory minimum sentencing laws."[23] The term "lynching" not only connects the current legal system to this country's legacies of racial violence but also aligns with some of the most recognized critiques of U.S. prisons. This expanding body of literature reveals how the criminalization of racial, sexual, and gender difference pervades our everyday practices and social configurations.[24] In concert, these formal and informal procedures create legal avenues for persecution, assault, and even murder while policies like mandatory minimums extend the reach and power of the state.

In Alexander's experience, as in many other cases of domestic violence, the mandatory minimum meant that her husband's history of abuse and the dire circumstances of her crime were irrelevant to her sentencing. The judge asserted that the decision was "out of [his] hands"—that he could not consider domestic violence as a mitigating circumstance.[25] Because survivors of domestic abuse are often criminalized for the actions they take in self-defense, and because Black women and other historically disadvantaged folks are more often seen and treated as criminals, policies like mandatory minimums serve as institutional reinforcement for the ongoing disenfranchisement of certain communities. In fact, mandatory minimums have allowed prosecutors to force guilty pleas; they can "load up" cases with unsubstantiated charges that carry extreme sentences to intimidate defendants into pleading guilty for lesser crimes.[26]

These intimidation tactics are also frequently applied to LGBTQ+ survivors, who must combat homophobic and transphobic assumptions. During the trial of the New Jersey 4—Venice Brown, Terrain Dandridge, Renata Hill, and Patreese Johnson—news outlets used sensationalist headlines tapping into the gender and race anxieties of the white middle class; for example: "Girls Gone Wilding," "Lesbian Gang Epidemic?" and "Attack of the Killer Lesbians."[27] Even the *New York Times* robbed the four of any agency with the headline, "Man Is Stabbed in Attack after Admiring a Stranger."[28] Despite video evidence that Buckle initiated the physical aggression, the four were found guilty. As in Alexander's trial, the prosecutors only needed to align the defendants with existing, ubiquitous representations of angry Black women and predatory, man-hating lesbians to flip public perceptions of perpetrator and victim.

Ky Peterson learned early on that such scripts denied him the supposed protections of the law. By his teen years, Peterson and his brothers all had encounters with law enforcement that taught them that they could never go to police for help. Before the assault that led to his conviction, Peterson had already been raped once, and police "could barely be bothered to file a report."[29] When officers arrived at the Peterson family home, they assumed that he and his brothers had committed armed robbery. Officers convinced themselves of a story wherein Peterson, whom they saw as a woman, had lured the assailant with promises of sex so the siblings could rob him. The nurse who administered Peterson's rape kit also misgendered him, determining that he "didn't act like a woman who had been raped."[30] The fact that legal and health professionals act with racist and cis-normative assumptions perpetuated not only the story of Peterson's assault but also the denial of his experience and pain afterward.

The experiences of Alexander, the New Jersey 4, and Ky Peterson are not aberrations but the norm. Black women and girls are twice as likely to be imprisoned as their white counterparts. Queer women are eight times as likely to be in prison as heterosexual women and more likely to experience sexual abuse as children and during incarceration.[31] Nearly 50 percent of Black trans women have been incarcerated. Once in prison, LGBQ folks are three times as likely to be sexually assaulted. For trans people, the rate of sexual assault is ten times that of cisgender people in the same facility. When transgender women are forced into the same carceral housing as cisgender men (as is often the case), their rate of sexual victimization becomes thirteen times that of cis people.[32]

The disparate experiences of incarceration and abuse are features of the system, not a bug. They are the result of a racist queer- and transphobic society in which LGBTQ+ children are far more likely to be ejected from their homes; of a dysfunctional foster care system in which many children grow up with unstable family lives; and of discriminatory policies in housing, health care, and employment that make it harder for LGBTQ+ folks and particularly QTPOC to secure food and shelter. When LGBTQ+ people of color, especially, are more likely to be mistreated at school and at home, they are placed at an inherent disadvantage in a meritocracy that values the sorts of educations afforded by white middle-class family formations. Every institution they encounter from childhood on was built to *assign* criminality as endemic to particular bodies—relegating many Black, Indigenous, and trans and queer folks to low-wage labor with limited economic mobility. The school-to-prison pipeline focuses on *removing* criminalized individuals from civic participation, denying the relevancy of their pasts or any hope for a future. Many, like Ky Peterson, are thus rightly skeptical that these same institutions would ever provide them any semblance of justice.

In direct defiance of carceral models of justice, Survived & Punished, Love & Protect, Freedom Overground, and other defenders of criminalized survivors have had to pursue alternative goals. Rather than seeking retribution for the survivors—which directs attention and resources to punishing offenders—these groups focus on the needs of survivors and empower them to direct their healing processes. For Marissa Alexander, this meant that her advocates maintained consistent dialogue with Alexander and her family and brought their reflections and updates to her supporters. The Chicago Alliance to Free Marissa Alexander (CAFMA) then channeled these insights into public education efforts that situated her story within systems of disenfranchisement. CAFMA members did not see their efforts as concluded when Alexander was released, instead committing to "supporting Marissa until her life was restored as much as possible."[33] Because Alexander was placed under home confinement, CAFMA raised funds to cover the additional expenses of her ankle monitoring. Their final hashtag, #UntilMarisssaIsFree, emphasized that "freedom" required not only release from prison but also the means to (re)build the life that abuse and incarceration had stolen from her.

Likewise, Freedom Overground, which began as the "Free Ky Project," also adapted its approach according to Peterson's wishes and needs. On their webpage, they explained, "Ky has faced retaliation from the DOC for the actions that he has taken to get medical care for trans inmates. Doing interviews cost him video visit privileges. Exposing negligent health care and putting the DOC under pressure has made him a target. His parole request was denied last Jan, his visitor requests have been denied, and even his Facebook was reported and permanently deleted."[34]

Respecting Peterson's wishes to "lay low" and avoid further retaliation from the Department of Correction, Freedom Overground shifted its tactics. Rather than campaigning explicitly in Peterson's name, they focused on developing programs for transgender prisoners and cultivating supportive networks and resources for transgender and gender-nonconforming people to build lives "above the underground economy."[35] In doing so, they not only provided support for Peterson upon his release in 2020 but also built the infrastructure to assist other trans and gender-nonconforming survivors. The creation of such structures is crucial for helping survivors like Peterson escape cycles of imprisonment, providing systems of mutual uplift when dominant institutions cannot be trusted.

Like Peterson and his team, the other survivors described here have also devoted their efforts to reimagining approaches to harm and reparation. Since her release, Marissa Alexander has taken consulting and speaking roles that address the mutual dependencies of domestic violence and the carceral system.[36] She has used her story as a rallying point, pulling together survivors of violence for mutual support and advocacy.[37] The organizers behind Free Marissa Now have channeled the lessons of their advocacy experiences to help other incarcerated survivors and create resources such as the *#SurvivedAndPunished* toolkit. Likewise, the New Jersey 4 have become vocal advocates for incarcerated survivors, speaking at colleges and universities, film festivals, and the National Convening of Black Lives.[38] Together, these efforts seek to protect women of color and trans and queer folks of color from life conditions that render them vulnerable to criminalization and imprisonment.

Through the lens of criminal justice, interpersonal violence is presumed to be pervasive and inevitable. Police and courts respond *after* the harm has already happened, and incarceration suggests the perpetrator cannot be redeemed but only removed from civil society. This system then enforces a narrative in which criminality belongs to certain bodies, and those bodies must be sequestered from the general public. The stories of Marissa Alexander, the New Jersey 4, Ky Peterson, and the advocacy groups that helped free them, however, expose these mechanisms as yet another arm of racist, misogynistic, and queer- and transphobic violence. They demonstrate how criminalization serves to remove troublesome Others from civic participation.

Rather than reinforce these logics, Survived and Punished, Love and Protect, Freedom Overground, and the survivors they support have prioritized creating livable worlds for those targeted by policing. S&P and L&P demonstrate how grassroots organizing can not only resist the wrongful conclusions of policing and courts but also uplift incarcerated survivors after their release. Their emphasis on "freedom" as self-determination and the means to build a life spotlights the roles that employment, health care, social networks, and other institutions play in criminalization. Likewise, Ky Peterson and Freedom Overground have worked to create the conditions for transgender survival both during and after incarceration, stressing how often trans people end up in criminal proceedings because of discriminatory living conditions that continually place them in precarious situations.

Conclusion

When Judge Aquilina lamented the limitations of her authority under the law, she also advised one of the young women who testified against Nassar, "Leave your pain here and go out and do your magnificent things."[39] The courtroom, however, was never made to witness the pain of survivors like Marissa Alexander. The officers of that court rarely see people like Ky Peterson as capable of magnificent things. Instead, these authorities remove Venice Brown, Terrain Dandridge, Renata Hill, and Patreese Johnson from their homes and families and rob them of critical years to develop relationships, careers, and full lives. Unlike the carceral solutions celebrated in prominent #MeToo narratives, the work of these survivors and their organizations aspires to create sustainable conditions for healing and thriving. Their stories demonstrate that policing and prisons perpetuate cycles of violence and that any lasting solution to rape culture will need to address its imbrications with racism, transphobia, and homophobia. Moreover, these survivors and organizations respond to violence as a systemic and social problem, rather than the sole province of individual offenders. Until this perspective is more widely accepted, Gerard Bryant is correct: our reactions to harm will be to isolate and contain; we will have prisons; we will have sexual abuse in prisons; and we will continue inflicting this pain.

Notes

1. Abigail Pesta, "What Nassar Judge Did Isn't Bias: It's Empowerment," *CNN*, January 25, 2020, https://www.cnn.com/2020/01/25/opinions/larry-nassar-judge-aquilina-wasnt-biased-pesta/index.html.

2. Elizabeth Bruenig, "Judge Rosemarie Aquilina's Real Message," *Washington Post*, January 25, 2018, https://www.washingtonpost.com/blogs/post-partisan/wp/2018/01/25/judge-rosemarie-aquilinas-real-message/.

3. Victoria Law, "City Worries Rules to Stop Thriving Rape Culture on Rikers Island Are Too 'Labor-Intensive,'" *Village Voice*, July 27, 2016, https://www.villagevoice.com/2016/07/27/city-worries-rules-to-stop-thriving-rape-culture-on-rikers-island-are-too-labor-intensive/.

4. Law, "City Worries Rules."

5. National Center for Transgender Equality, *LGBTQ People behind Bars: A Guide to Understanding the Issues Facing Transgender Prisoners and their Legal Rights*, October 2018, https://transequality.org/transpeoplebehindbars.

6. Michelle Alexander, *The New Jim Crow: Mass Incarceration in the Age of Colorblindness* (New York: New Press, 2010); Angela J. Davis, ed. *Policing the Black Man: Arrest, Prosecution, and Imprisonment* (New York: Pantheon Books, 2017); Beth Richie, *Arrested Justice: Black Women, Violence, and America's Prison Nation* (New York: NYU Press, 2012); Ersula Ore, *Lynching: Violence, Rhetoric, and American Identity* (Jackson: University of Mississippi Press, 2019).

7. Ruth Wilson Gilmore, *Golden Gulag: Prisons, Surplus, Crisis, and Opposition in Globalizing California*, American Crossroads 21 (Berkeley: University of California Press, 2007): Alex S. Vitale, *The End of Policing* (New York: Verso, 2017); Isabel Wilkerson, *Caste: The Origins of Our Discontents* (New York: Random House, 2020); Alexander, *New Jim Crow*; Ore, *Lynching*.

8. Dorothy E. Roberts, *Killing the Black Body: Race, Reproduction, and the Meaning of Liberty* (New York: Vintage Books, 1997); Patricia Hill Collins, *Black Feminist Thought: Knowledge, Consciousness, and the Politics of Empowerment* (New York: Routledge, 2000); Monique W. Morris, *Pushout: The Criminalization of Black Girls in Schools* (New York: New Press, 2016).

9. Mark Anthony Neal, *Looking for Leroy: Illegible Black Masculinities* (New York: NYU Press, 2013); Davis, *Policing the Black Man*; Jared Sexton, *Black Masculinity and the Cinema of Policing* (New York: Palgrave Macmillan, 2017).

10. Andrea Ritchie, *Invisible No More*: *Police Violence against Black Women and Women of Color* (Boston: Beacon Press, 2017).

11. Kimberlé Crenshaw, "Demarginalizing the Intersection of Race and Sex: A Black Feminist Critique of Antidiscrimination Doctrine, Feminist Theory and Antiracist Politics," *University of Chicago Legal Forum* 1, no. 8 (1989): 139–167.

12. Tarana Burke, "#MeToo Founder Tarana Burke on the Rigorous Work that Still Lies Ahead," *Variety* (blog), September 25, 2018, https://variety.com/2018/biz/features/tarana-burke-metoo-one -year-later-1202954797/; Liz Rowley, "#MeToo Founder Says the Movement Has Lost Its Way," *The Cut*, October 23, 2018, https://www.thecut.com/2018/10/tarana-burke-me-too-founder -movement-has-lost-its-way.html.

13. Alisa Bierria, Mariame Kaba, Essence McDowell, Hyejin Shim, and Stacy Suh, eds. *#SurvivedAndPunished: Survivor Defense as Abolitionist Praxis*, http://www.survivedandpunished.org/sp -toolkit.html, 2.

14. Bierria et al., *#SurvivedAndPunished*, 2.

15. Bierria et al., *#SurvivedAndPunished*, 7.

16. Bierria et al., *#SurvivedAndPunished*, 6.

17. Nicole Pasulka, "How 4 Gay Black Women Fought Back against Sexual Harassment—and Landed in Jail," *NPR Code Switch*, June 30, 2015, https://www.npr.org/sections/codeswitch/2015/06/30/418634390/how-4-gay-black-women-fought-back-against-a-sexual-harasser-and-landed-in-jail.

18. Pasulka, "How 4 Gay Black Women."

19. Although most reports refer to the New Jersey 4 as "women," Terrain Dandridge now uses both he/him and she/her pronouns. See Out in the Night, "Meet the NJ4," 2020, http://www.outinthenight.com/meet-the-nj4/.

20. In accordance with Peterson's wishes (see Devin-Norelle), I've minimized details about Peterson's assault to deemphasize that phase of his story and to direct attention to the futures he is building.

21. Bierria et al., *#SurvivedAndPunished*, 7; Dean Spade and Hope Dector, *Ky Peterson*, Survived and Punished and the Barnard Center for Research on Women, 2017, https://www.youtube.com/watch?time_continue=48&v=W7ySbCx_SwE.

22. Spade and Dector, *Ky Peterson*.

23. Bierria et al., *#SurvivedAndPunished*, 7.

24. Beth Ritchie, *Compelled to Crime: The Gender Entrapment of Battered Black Women* (New York: Routledge, 1996); Angela J. Davis, *Are Prisons Obsolete?* (New York: Seven Stories Press, 2003): Dean Spade, *Normal Life: Administrative Violence, Critical Trans Politics, and the Limits of Law* (Durham: Duke University Press, 2015). Eric Stanley and Nat Smith, eds., *Captive Genders: Trans Embodiment and the Prison Industrial Complex*, exp. 2nd ed. (Oakland, CA: AK Press, 2015); INCITE! Women of Color against Violence, ed., *Color of Violence: The INCITE! Anthology* (Durham: Duke University Press, 2016); Victor M. Rios, *Human Targets: Schools, Police, and the Criminalization of*

Latino Youth (Chicago: University of Chicago Press, 2017); Ore, *Lynching*.

25. Mitch Stacy, "Woman Gets 20 Years for Firing Warning Shot," *Washington Times*, May 19, 2012, https://www.washingtontimes .com/news/2012/may/19/woman-gets-20-years-firing-warning -shot/.

26. Alexander, *New Jim Crow*, 88.

27. Out in the Night, "Meet the NJ4."

28. Cara Buckley and Kate Hammer, "Man Is Stabbed in Attack after Admiring a Stranger," *New York Times*, August 19, 2006, https://www.nytimes.com/2006/08/19/nyregion/19stab.html.

29. Sunniyie Brydum and Mitch Kellaway, "This Black Trans Man Is in Prison for Killing His Rapist," *The Advocate*, April 8, 2015, http://www.advocate.com/politics/transgender/2015/04/08/black -trans-man-prison-killing-his-rapist.

30. Alison Turkos and Shivana Jorawar, "We Survived Rape: Don't Use Us to Support the Police," *Cosmopolitan*, July 8, 2020, https://www.cosmopolitan.com/politics/a33216997/sexual-assault -survivors-police-abolition/.

31. Ilan H. Meyer, Andrew R. Flores, Lara Stemple, Adam P. Romero, Bianca D. M. Wilson, and Jody L. Herman, "Incar- ceration Rates and Traits of Sexual Minorities in the United States: National Inmate Survey, 2011–2012," *American Journal of Public Health* 107, no. 2 (February 2017): 267–273.

32. National Center for Transgender Equality, "LGBTQ People Behind Bars."

33. Ayanna Banks Harris, quoted in Bierria et al., *#SurvivedAndPun- ished*, 27.

34. Freedom Overground Corp, "Ky Peterson FAQ," https://www .freedomoverground.org/ky-peterson-campaign.

35. Freedom Overground Corp, "Ky Peterson FAQ."

36. Christine Hauser, "Florida Woman Whose 'Stand Your Ground' Defense Was Rejected Is Released," *New York Times*,

February 7, 2017, https://www.nytimes.com/2017/02/07/us
/marissa-alexander-released-stand-your-ground.html.

37. Marissa Alexander, "Walking in My Truth: An Interview with
    Marissa Alexander," *The Monument Quilt*, March 19, 2019,
    https://themonumentquilt.org/walking-in-my-truth-an
    -interview-with-marissa-alexander/.

38. Out in the Night, "Meet the NJ4."

39. Scott Cacciola, "Victims in Larry Nassar Abuse Case Find a
    Fierce Advocate: The Judge," *New York Times*, January 23, 2018,
    https://www.nytimes.com/2018/01/23/sports/larry-nassar
    -rosemarie-aquilina-judge.html.

13

"Oppression Was at My Doorstep from Birth"

A Conversation on Prison Abolition

DOMINIQUE MORGAN AND TREVOR HOPPE

TREVOR: Dominique, thank you so much for joining me to discuss the connections between mass incarceration, prison abolition, and sexuality and gender for readers. Maybe we could start just by talking a little bit about Black and Pink and the abolitionist work that you all do?

DOMINIQUE: At Black and Pink, you look at our mission statement, it talks about dismantling any barriers of oppression that are impacting LGBTQ+ people or people who identify as living with HIV and AIDS. We create answers and initiatives and innovate at Black and Pink with the idea that everyone deserves access to whatever they think is going to give them access to their best life.

When we talk about abolition, so many people look at abolition from perspective of just prison abolition—jails, detention centers. We want to abolish systems of oppression. Jails and prisons are in there, yes. But if we close all the jails and prisons today, I don't have anywhere to house these people. I don't have food to feed them. I don't have medication for their needs. These are real things. And so how can we dismantle those systems?

And we are people-centered. And that means that we believe that the answers lie in community and that community is the ultimate answer to system divestment. And we're just trying to build out initiatives that make healthier individuals, that make healthier communities that get us to this space where community can lean on, grow from this reciprocal process within community and systems, and the ways that system shows up can be put to the side.

TREVOR: A lot of my students have a passion for thinking about inequality and mass incarceration, particularly when it comes to Black communities in the United States. But many LGBTQ people—especially white LGBTQ people—don't really have a strong understanding of why these issues of the criminal justice system are important issues for queer communities. What would you say to one of my young, progressive, queer white students who hasn't yet connected those dots?

DOMINIQUE: I think in the space that allows me to offer grace. So let me start there, in someone's experience or inability to see it. . . . They haven't had to—they don't see it because it doesn't affect them because of their whiteness. And the ability for you to even lean into the impact of oppression will only probably shift if you are a cisgender white male that's heavier, or a cisgender white male that's queer that's over 30, or a cisgender white male that is over 30, heavier, and you're poor. That's when you figure out when you go on Grindr and they say no fats or femmes—that's when you recognize about oppression. And that's cool because many of us, our first time of *aha* is because it landed at our doorsteps. For someone like myself, oppression was at my doorstep from birth. I think that's one piece.

I would say to then look at your own life and look at areas where, based on the identities you carry, access, or reach, possibly has been more difficult for you or it's been impeded. Look at those spaces. For female cisgender, lesbians, they're easily able, even the TERF amongst them, are easily able to talk about the oppression of being a woman in this world. For a TERF, the gag is that they want to own oppression—you don't want to share oppression. Girl, whatever.

But I think starting with identities and your experiences and be like, "Look, these are times where simply because of who I was, because of who I love, or because of how I've shown up, that's happened."

And then I'm always saying, start with yourself, but don't stop with yourself. Look at history. Don't go out there collecting Black friends, sitting there like, "Tell me about your struggle." You don't need to do that because you can look at the history of our communities to dig into it. Like myself as a Black trans woman, yes, I see it around me every day but often it's by reading or watching a documentary where I can really grasp the history of the oppression of my people. Oppression doesn't hit the way it should when you're looking at the present. You got to look at the history of it.

Last but not least, I try to affirm the valid fear, which I think a lot of this comes out of people feeling if we're talking about somebody else, we're not going to be talking about me.

TREVOR: Maybe it's that inability to deal with more issues than one at a time. I feel that with my students sometimes. They come to class really focused and want to talk about drug offenses and nonviolent offenses. And anything beyond that is very scary territory for them. And I see this with LGBT organizations as well. They want nothing to do with criminal justice reform or especially sex offense policy. Why do you think that extending the national conversation on criminal justice reform into the realm of sexuality is so difficult?

DOMINIQUE: I think one of the reasons is that people think if we abolish these systems—and if we do away with the good and bad dichotomy—that people are going to lose a lot of their privilege. A lot of people really like this idea that you can say, "I've never been a felon. I've never been in jail. I did go to jail, but it was a DUI; it's not like I murdered anybody." Those types of things people say create levels of good and bad, who deserves and who doesn't deserve. And I think that human piece where people struggle with is, "How do you get to identify as a good person when everybody is a good person?" Trevor, you have a PhD. Let's say for instance, you busted your ass for that PhD. Fair?

TREVOR: Fair.

DOMINIQUE: The stories I've heard people in a PhD program, that's some shit.

TREVOR: It took seven years.

DOMINIQUE: Imagine if everybody in the country was handed a PhD right now. Now you believe in equality; you believe in fairness and abolition but you will be like, "No bitch, I know you not." You know what I'm saying? Give me my student loan money. All these things, because your status as someone who has a PhD in the world you work in puts you in a space of power and influence. Now, you may weaponize that power and influence for good and have the best of intentions, but let's be clear, no one goes through 10 years of school to be like everybody else. Fair?

TREVOR: Fair.

DOMINIQUE: Okay. That's the same thing with these. That's the same thing when folks are like, "Oh let's talk about petty crimes," because they could possibly see themselves doing that. They can see themselves with it. But they don't want to ever think that there could be a situation where they're put in harm's way to where they may have to kill someone, where they could be so poor, they could have so much going around them where you're walking down the street and you haven't eaten and you see somebody's personal message to that car, and it's like, "Listen, I'm hungry. I'm not thinking about the other person hungry right now." They can't put themselves there because they just can't, because they just can't imagine being oppressed that way.

I am not oblivious to the fact that most people love my story because it's a comeback story. If I got up and failed ten times, wouldn't nobody care about what I've done. "Okay, girl, you messed up ten times. You might want to get it in order." People love that I came home from prison after all this time, and now I'm this national leader and all that. That's what they love. We love those movies. The triumphant moments where it's just like, "You have a little struggle," the gumption. I think that's a huge piece.

I think the other part is that we indoctrinate each other for our whole lives about what is good and what is bad. If *Law and Order SVU*—and I'm an *SVU* fan—but if that show was about DUIs for twenty years, would nobody watch that.

Everything we see, the worst is murdering somebody. The unforgivable. I was, at the top of the pandemic, I was on an *SVU*-watching marathon. I'm like, "Girl, he'd have got three years for that." I'll sit there and sometimes it'll be like, "That prison sentence will never happen." But [these shows] tell people what you can come back from and what you can't—what is something someone can do that will make it okay for us as a society to throw them away. And what are the things that someone can do we can be like, "You know what, you kind of messed up, but I'm going to give you a chance to be better?"

And I think those are the two avenues that usually intersect when I'm having conversations with people. Aya Gruber has this book about feminist abolitionists who struggle in the space of sexual harm. They can get all the way—murder, all the things—and then they hit that brick wall.

And that means we have to do that internal work to divest, abolish this idea that people are 100% good, that people are 100% bad. Ursula [in *The Little Mermaid*] wasn't a bitch. Ursula was just like, "Ariel, you're always in my shit. Girl I told you to leave me alone. I gave you an NDA; you signed it. And I just want your voice because that's what it gave." I always think about the villains that have been sold to us as villains our whole lives. And you look back and be like, "Were they a villain? Were they?"

You know what I'm saying? Alice in Wonderland messing with people's stuff. If I was the Queen of Hearts, go off with your head too, get out of my shit. I know it seems petty, but these are all the things that teach us who we are, that teach us about what it is to be good people; from fairytales on, it teaches us. Well, you look at even characteristics where the darker-skinned person is the bad person. The girl with the dark hair is the bad person—all these things, these little characteristics. Why do you think so many people dye their hair blonde?

Let's be clear; this is real shit. And so, to go back to your initial question, Trevor, if we divest from all of that, we would have a world where people would be really struggling to figure out who is going to affirm and tell them that they're good. And I don't think folks want to invest in the therapy and the shadow work to figure that out in themselves.

TREVOR: You kind of segued nicely to these questions about what you were calling the wall that we hit around issues of sexual violence—that you can get through conversations about murder and people who commit violent offenses. And then you get to sex offenses, and it's just this wall. And I know that we've talked a little bit before about your own journey and coming to that wall and getting past that wall. What challenges did you face? What allowed you to get past that roadblock for you in thinking about sexual violence?

DOMINIQUE: The first big push was working with Zephyr Williams, our deputy director of community organizational health here at Black and Pink. Zeph and I met in the summer of 2017. And I remember walking in. This was pre-transition but even as a professional life person, my attire was khakis and a polo. And so, I walk in, and Zeph was just sitting there in like a suit, snatched to the heavens, and was just so pulled together. So pulled together that I did not think that he was a part of the formerly incarcerated subgroup, because in my experience up to that point, people who have been incarcerated don't look that *together*. Right? So, I thought he was a part of the planning team or an attorney or somebody and I'm like, "Who is this?" And we run around the room, and we started talking and he unapologetically brought up the sex offense registry.

And I was just like, "What's going on?" And I just remember, I didn't say anything. And then over that weekend, we just really were drawn to each other, and we had some great conversations. I love how fierce they were in space. Honestly, everyone there, I just became in awe of them because I had never met so many people who've been in the system who were so powerful and so dope. And we could talk about work stuff, but we could also talk about how to make a prison spread. And I didn't feel weird or awkward among people. We became real friends and then family. And that was the first moment I was pushed. And I remember, we were talking about how Zeph has two master's degrees, is brilliant, but had never had a paid job because of being impacted by the registry. And I was like, "That can't be fair."

Because my barrier around the sexual harm piece wasn't that they can't get better. It was that most times they don't. It started with Zeph—Zeph was the perfect example. For me, in my mind, this person is doing everything right. And they still can't get a piece of opportunity. This isn't fair. And then finding out more and more about how the registry not only impacts people in Nebraska but then I started to hear about how the registry was so different and sometimes so much more harmful other places. I listened to Robert Suttle talking about them putting markers on your ID about HIV and AIDS when you're on the registry. Finding out about in Louisiana at that time, that you could literally be in your home with your partner and be charged with an indecent crime and be on the registry.

When I started to learn how the registry was weaponized against Black people, all these other things. There was so much I did not know, and I had made so many judgments based on what I didn't know, which is dangerous.

Another piece that made me realize is that I was raised by the system. So of course, I had adopted many of the values and beliefs of the system. And I was 14, 15, in a group home in Nebraska and I remember how the staff would talk about these 10, 9-year-old boys who were there for sexual harm—and how they would talk about how these kids would always be the same. That's how I first heard about it.

The next step was the fact that, when I became the executive director of Black and Pink, no matter who was a Black and Pink member, no matter their charges, whatever: I had signed up to be their executive director. I had signed up to be their leader. I signed up for it. And they deserve the best of me. The only way that I could show up the way I wanted to show up was a divestment of asking people [about their charges]. A big culture thing in prison is when you meet somebody who's been locked up or you meet somebody in the community or the streets who've been locked, you be like, "What was you locked up for?"

That's the norm to ask about charges. It's because people want to know who's there for a sex crime and who's not. But that's even a thing now in our work where we were formerly incarcerated—we've been somebody [who] would want to know how long they were locked up and this and that to validate their experience. I just divested from that when I became the ED. I don't want to know. I said this earlier today, I care more about your sign than what your charge is. I care more about if you're one of those people that puts mayonnaise on your fries.

The last step was really doing a lot of work and being able to call off the lawsuit that I had against the State of Nebraska and the correctional officer that I experienced sexual harm from at the end of my prison sentence. And realizing that the system was very comfortable positioning this man for power and access to be able to engage with harm with my body, but the system didn't want to be accountable for the harm that happened.

And I had a moment where I was just like, "If this man is the only person in this lawsuit, it will substantiate for people that one person makes harm happen." And I, at that point, December of 2019, I didn't believe that anymore. And it wasn't that I didn't believe it because I don't hold that man accountable for what he did to me, but it's because I know he did not do that on his own. There was many, many things in my life, many harms that happened in my life, even lack of information about things that would have possibly changed what that experience would have been with him.

What was I going to get out of this process? And so, that took a lot of personal conversation and divestment, and I think the most grief I had. I remember just crying, calling my friend Ashley and crying on the phone. Wasn't because of being sad about giving up the lawsuit. It was because I realized that the entire time I was in the system, nobody was ever really responsible for me being safe. Because if anyone was ever responsible, it wouldn't have been so hard to hold someone accountable in ten years.

If I didn't have autonomy, I don't have choice. These laws, these systems are set up to where if someone's in the system, they just do what you tell them to do. Then who's my protector? Who makes sure I'm okay? And then if I'm not okay, who's accountable for that not happening? And I realized that my body, for the majority of my life at that point, had never been protected.

The most protected I have ever felt was as an abolitionist who leaned on community and not systems. I'm going to keep on leaning on community. Even the times that I have doubts or concerns, or I waiver. I think in the space of sexual harm, I honestly, some days have to rededicate myself to it where I see something on the news.

TREVOR: No, I feel that. And it's almost how I feel right now about the George Floyd murder trial. Well, I'm glad that this police officer's being held to account. At the same time, it should be the police department that is on trial, not necessarily just this individual. And it's frustrating that our system of justice think so individually when these problems are fundamentally structural. How do you navigate wanting to see justice or at least some form of justice done when you believe the system is so fundamentally broken that you don't think it's even maybe possible?

DOMINIQUE: Well, for me, it's that I have stopped depending on the system to give me anything that looks like restoration and transformation. And I don't think justice is a real thing. I just don't believe in it anymore. I know that a system isn't going to bring that to me.

We will send somebody to twenty years in prison, but they will not make somebody apologize to you. The things that make me feel better about harm that's happened to me, the courts don't even have power over. And I think that is a piece, I think poverty and many of the oppressive systems that Black people experience, they make them think the system is necessary because you've gotten this money. There will never be enough money that is equivalent enough to what George would have been to the people in his life. $27 million, when you think of taxes, half of that is gone. Once you get down to it, $10 million for you murdering this man in front of everyone? I'm good. You know what I'm saying? That doesn't equate.

And two, you all are going to try to put the problem on this man when, like I said about the corporal that sexually harmed me. Derek Chauvin had been a part of the police force for years. You cannot tell me that's the first time he's done something harmful to somebody that day. Who didn't reply to the report? Who didn't believe the complaints? Who positioned him to be in power that day to call that harm? And I think the reason that won't ever happen, Trevor, [is that] if we affirm that most community harms happen because community and systems position people to cause harm, then we all will be accountable for the healing to happen.

And people love being like, "That is not my business. Oh, I didn't do that." Well, let's talk about that. People think being accountable means that you're bad. I think for me, accountability is exciting because I can look at an issue and know my part of it. I can do some self-interrogation. Because if I buy into it, all or nothing, I'm always going to be comforted with the idea that "Well, this person committed this crime, so put them in the electric chair and that addresses the issue." When I know that's not real.

TREVOR: Well, that leads me to just one last question, which is, If you were able to wave a magic wand and to get queer communities to respond to sexual harm differently or find other ways to deal with that than calling the police, what do you think that could look in practice? How can queer communities respond to sexual harm?

DOMINIQUE: I'm always like, "Okay, well, this is the current process. Let's look at how this has worked." Look at when sexual harm has happened in queer communities. Let's look at the data that shows how helpful the police have been. Let's look at the data that looks at the impact—if these people were ever even charged. More times than not, I know queer folks who have reported harm and the fact that they are gay, there's just no belief that they could ever be raped by any man—or folks who are doing sex work who are being sexually harmed in that time. "Well, you're a prostitute. What do you mean that somebody raped you?"

And so, I think we need to look at, if you're telling me this system is the best you got, how has it shown up? And I think we know what that answer will be.

I think the next piece is looking at, what is our accountability in how we support sexual harm happening in queer communities. This idea of the younger you are, the more vulnerable you are. I was 16 years old and my first partner was 21. And we don't talk enough about how the queer community is oversexualized to the point that we believe that sometimes our only benefit is being sexual that way. When are we calling out the harm that happens? You're in the bar, you know this guy is drunk as hell. Why are you letting this child go to the bathroom by themselves? We know what it is; it's just real. And we don't talk about it enough.

And I think last, but not least, dreaming about what we can create that brings us a safety experience that we want to have. If we are honest, the system will never bring this to fruition for us. People want to feel safe engaging in certain things. The police are never going to make me feel safe as a Black trans woman going on an app, going on Plenty of Fish to date someone. I can't call the cops and be like, "Listen, I'm going to go meet this guy. Police officer, can I share my location with you? And if you don't hear from me in an hour, will you call and check on me?" I can't do that with the police. I do that with my friends. That's how I feel safe.

The police can't give me that. What does it mean to be safe? What does it feel like to be safe? What needs to be in place? We don't talk about that enough.

What's existing that feels safe and what's missing? And what can we create that is not birthed from systems that inherently harm us? What can we do?

It may be scary, but what we do know is, this thing, this girl over here, she don't. Stonewall is a thing because police tried to take us away. It wasn't about two queens in the street fighting over a man. You know what I'm saying? The police were trying to kill us and arrest us because of who we were.

How is it possible that the roots of our liberation are based in pushing back on the police, and we think because we're fifty-two years from Stonewall that now we've reached a point where the police are now our buddies? Quit telling brown and Black folks, quit telling queer folks that it would be better for them to become a part of the system. I know lesbian cops and they full of shit too. Because one of two things happen. If you go through the system and shake it up, try to dismantle it, the system becomes scared of you and pushes you out. Or you go in there with those intentions, but you do want to get along. And you want to be able to make a living. And so, you assimilate. One or the other.

And so we need to stop saying that as well. Oh, it's not the system, just not enough Black people. We don't have enough gay people. You can do all the diversity sessions with the police you want to around queerness, but do they know how to handle it when they go to the park and somebody is getting a blowjob behind a tree? That's what I want to talk about. I don't care about the other shit. I think that's the biggest thing is, does it work? If it hasn't worked, what can work? And anything that's going to work is going to be centered in us.

Acknowledgments

First and foremost, we must thank all the brilliant contributors to this volume. Their commitment to thinking through the hoary, "unsafe" issues of sex, consent, and harm made this book possible. Each contributor has made us, as editors and as everyday queer people, think differently and critically about consent and queer community-making. We are indebted to them.

We are especially thankful to be able to include the words of Mistress Velvet, a radical Black feminist who dared to imagine and put into practice a sexual politics few among us could emulate. They are gone far too soon. The world—particularly the communities of trans and genderqueer folks and sex workers they worked so hard to support, educate, and organize—is not the same without them.

Beyond the writers here, we must also thank the editors of Q+ Public, Jeffrey Escoffier and E. G. Crichton. We are particularly grateful for the support we had from Jeffrey before his passing. His enthusiasm for this book and all the other books in the Q+ Public series was infectious and inspiring. Jeffrey was an intellectual pioneer and helped to shape so much of what we know as queer and LGBTQ studies, this book included. We hope that the timely, short volumes E.G. and Jeffrey have helped usher to publication will be immensely valuable to generating urgently needed conversations for queer communities everywhere. We also thank Don Romesburg, who initially approached us with the idea for this volume, and other members of the Q+ Public editorial board for their encouragement and feedback. Finally, we would also like to thank Lisa DeBoer, for compiling the index to this volume.

Beyond this volume itself, we are grateful for those who came before us who provided the foundation to speak the words in this book into existence. Black feminists such as Cathy Cohen, Barbara Smith, and Patricia Hill Collins inspire many of the authors in this book. Sex-positive feminists like Gayle Rubin and Patrick Califia provide many of us with the tools to understand the radical potential of sex. Queer social theorists like David Halperin, Judith Butler, Rod Ferguson, José Esteban Munoz, Audre Lorde, Eve Sedgewick, Gloria Anzaldúa, and Michael Warner also help many of us critically resist heteronormative calls to conform.

We must also thank the many other radical activists and sexual pioneers who have put their lives on the line in the name of pleasure and sexual ethics. Organizations like the Combahee River Collective and SisterSong demanded space for Black women in movements for gender and reproductive justice. We are especially thankful to collectives like INCITE! not only for their efforts to end state and community violence against women, gender-nonconforming, and trans people of color but also for providing a predecessor to this book with their 2016 anthology. Organizations like SAMOIS, the Gay Liberation Front, and Queer Nation fought to keep movements for queer people sexy and sex-positive. The many decades of work by these activists and countless others we have not named have made it possible to speak the "unsafe words" in this volume.

Notes on Contributors

BLU BUCHANAN (they/them) is a qualitative and historical scholar, employing methods ranging from archival analysis to oral history and interviews. Their research focuses on the role of violence in everyday life, which informs their twin research trajectories: (1) whiteness and masculinity as projects shaping intracommunal violence in the LGBT community and (2) the practices and habits that Black trans folks develop to resist and decenter violence in their everyday lives.

SHANTEL GABRIEAL BUGGS (she/her) is an assistant professor of sociology and African American studies at Florida State University. Her research explores race, ethnicity and racism, gender, intimacy, and digital space, with a focus on relationship formation, interracial sex and romance, online dating, and multiracial identity. In addition to organizing workshops on combating sexual violence in academia, she writes about the representation of race, gender, and sexuality in popular culture.

ALEXANDER CHEVES (he/him) has been writing about sexual health, queer relationships, and LGBTQ+ culture for a decade. He now writes the "Last Call" column for *Out Magazine* and runs the popular sex advice blog "Love, Beastly," known for its frank, unflinching answers to questions about queer sex. Cheves is a recipient of a 2021 Excellence in Journalism award from the National Lesbian and Gay Journalists Association and, in 2021, was named to the Out 100. His book, *My Love Is a Beast: Confessions*, is an erotic memoir sharing the unvarnished truth of his queer sex life—a classic coming-of-age story with sharply different details gathered through his tour of America's gay meccas.

ANAHI RUSSO GARRIDO (she/they) is an associate professor in gender, women's, and sexuality studies and serves as department chair and director of the Gender Institute for Teaching and Advocacy (GITA) at Metropolitan State University of Denver. She/they is the coeditor of *Building Feminist Movements and Organizations* and a dozen journal articles, chapters, and training manuals. Garrido is also the author of *Tortilleras Negotiating Intimacy: Love, Friendship and Sex in Queer Mexico City* and is currently working on a project on racial justice, care practices, and meditation.

GLORIA GONZÁLEZ-LÓPEZ (she/her) holds the C. B. Smith Sr. Centennial Chair #1 in US-Mexico Relations and is professor of sociology at the University of Texas at Austin. She is the author of *Family Secrets: Stories of Incest and Sexual Violence in Mexico* and *Erotic Journeys: Mexican Immigrants and their Sex Lives*. She is a couples and family therapist by training and has worked with Latina immigrant women with histories of sexual violence. She is a consultant for professionals working in sexual violence prevention and eradication, and treatment programs in grassroots organizations and academic institutions in Mexico. She received the 2021 Simon-Gagnon Lifetime Achievement Award from the American Sociological Association, Sexualities Section.

TREVOR HOPPE (he/him) is assistant professor of sociology at UNC Greensboro. His research examines the social control of sexuality by institutions of law, public health, and medicine. He is the author of the Lambda Literary Award–winning book, *Punishing Disease: HIV and the Criminalization of Sickness*. That book tracks the rise and application of HIV-specific criminal statutes in the United States, demonstrating how fear and stigma mixed with homophobia, racism, and anti-sex work ideologies to create the perfect storm for HIV criminalization. He is also the coeditor, with David Halperin, of *The War on Sex*, which examines the rise of punitive policies toward sex.

V. JO HSU (they/them) is an assistant professor of rhetoric and writing, a core faculty member in the Center for Asian American Studies, and a faculty affiliate of the LGBTQ Studies Program at the University of Texas at Austin. They are the author of *Constellating Home: Trans and Queer Asian American Rhetorics*. Their research examines the role of storytelling in enforcing and resisting structural inequalities, and their writing has appeared in major disciplinary journals and been nominated for a Pushcart Prize. You can access most of their work via www.vjohsu.com.

ANGELA JONES (she/they) is professor of sociology at Farmingdale State College, State University of New York. Jones's research interests include African American political thought and protest, sex work, race, gender, sexuality, feminist theory, and queer methodologies and theory. Jones is the author of nine books including *Camming: Money, Power, and Pleasure in the Sex Industry*; many scholarly articles in peer-reviewed journals; and pieces in the mainstream press.

MARK S. KING (he/him) has been an international voice for those living with HIV since he tested positive in 1985, only weeks after the HIV antibody test became publicly available. His enormously influential blog, "My Fabulous Disease," has been honored many times and won the 2020 GLAAD Media Award. King is also the author of *A Place like This*, his personal chronicle of his years in Los Angeles during the dawn of the AIDS crisis. He attributes his longevity to being an empowered and informed advocate, the love of a good man, and double-chocolate brownies made from scratch.

JAMES McMASTER (he/him) is assistant professor of gender and women's studies and Asian American studies at the University of Wisconsin–Madison, where he is also affiliated with the program in Interdisciplinary Theatre Studies. Through trans/queer, feminist, and crip analyses of Asian American cultural production and movement organizing, his research examines how Asian Americans have used aesthetic means to challenge and endure anti-Asian violence. His writing has appeared in the *Journal of Asian American Studies*, *American Quarterly*, *Journal of Dramatic Theory and Criticism*, and *Teen Vogue*.

DOMINIQUE MORGAN (she/her) is the executive director of Black and Pink National. She is a Black trans woman who experienced incarceration as a young person and as an adult and leads the organization from a strong transformative justice and reproductive justice standpoint as a community healer and a sexual health educator. Dominique's experiences and leadership ensure that Black and Pink's programming is conducted from a trauma-informed approach. Instead of asking, "What do we need to do to fix you?" its staff members ask, "What have you experienced?" and "What does success look like for you?" This builds a pathway to sustainability because their investment lives in those they serve and the solutions they dictate.

DON (D. S.) TRUMBULL (he/him) has had a passion for photography for the past twenty-four years. His portfolio consists of a wide range of subject matter, including landscapes, wildlife, nature, underwater, and portraiture photography. It is this versatility that allows Trumbull to bring a unique creativity to his leather+kink+fetish photography work as showcased in this book. This portraiture work within the leather community has remained his primary focus for the past eight years. You can find Trumbull's work displayed in national LGBTQI publications such as *The Advocate*, promotional material for LGBTQI events and products, and portraiture work of titleholders on the stage of the regional leather competitions, International Mister Bootblack competition, and International Mister Leather competition.

MISTRESS VELVET (she/they) was a sex worker and human rights advocate who fought tirelessly for the rights of Black people, sex workers, and transgender people. In her practice as Chicago's premier African Dominatrix, she required her cis white male clients to read and write essays about Black feminist theory. She earned an MA degree in women's and gender studies (with a focus on African diaspora studies) from UNC Greensboro and a BA in women's studies from UNC Chapel Hill.

JANE WARD (she/her) is professor of feminist studies at University of California, Santa Barbara, where she teaches courses in feminist, queer, and heterosexuality studies. She is author of the books *The Tragedy of Heterosexuality*; *Not Gay:*

Sex between Straight White Men; and *Respectably Queer: Diversity Culture in LGBT Activist Organizations.* Her current research focuses on the differences between paid and unpaid sexual labor. She is also an urban gardener, an antiracist organizer, and a parent to one potbelly pig, nine chickens, one cat, and one human child.

Index

Page numbers in italics refer to illustrations.

Velvet, Mistress, 9–10, 95–100
victim-blaming, 12
victimhood, politics of, 13, 160–163

Walker, Alice, 100
Ward, Jane, 8
Weinstein, Harvey, 158
white people: cis-heterosexual
    submissive men, 9–10, 95–100;
    gay men, 13, 44–45, 56; victim-
    hood of white women, 157–158,
    163. *See also* race
white supremacy, 30, 35, 99–100.
    See also racism
Williams, Zephyr, 181–182
women: comfort with bodies, 85–86;
    "no means no" model and, 48;
    politics of sex and, 1–2; power

and, 30; sexual pleasure, 65–71;
    systemic violence against, 50–51
    (*see also* domestic violence; sexual
    harm/violence). *See also* Black
    trans women; Black women;
    heterosexual sex; lesbians;
    #MeToo movement; women of
    color
Women against Pornography
    (organization), 1
women of color, 12; criminal justice
    system and, 158–169; fetishization
    of, 97–99, 131–134; heterosexual
    sex and, 66. *See also* Black trans
    women; Black women; race
Wu, Cynthia, 147

Zimmerman, George, 163